Take Your Bike!

Family Rides in the Finger Lakes and Genesee Valley Region

Take Your Bike!
Family Rides in the Finger Lakes
and Genesee Valley Region

By Rich and Sue Freeman

Footprint Press
Fishers, New York 14453
http://www.footprintpress.com

Other books available from Footprint Press:

Take A Hike! Family Walks in the Rochester Area
Take A Hike! Family Walks in the Finger Lakes
& Genesee Valley Region
Take Your Bike! Family Rides in the Rochester Area
Bruce Trail – An Adventure Along the Niagara Escarpment
Alter – A Simple Path to Emotional Wellness

Published in the United States of America by Footprint Press

Copy Edited by Maralyn E. Kaufman, Ph.D.
Cover Design by Tamara L. Dever, TLC Graphics
Maps by Rich Freeman
Pictures by Rich & Sue Freeman
Cover picture by Rich Freeman

ISBN 0-9656974-4-4

Manufactured in the United States of America

Library of Congress Catalog Card Number: 99-90039

Every effort has been made to provide accurate and up-to-date trail descriptions in this book. Hazards are noted where known. Users of this book are reminded that they alone are responsible for their own safety when on any trail or road and that they use the routes described in this book at their own risk.

The authors, publishers, and distributors of this book assume no responsibility for any injury, misadventure, or loss occurring from use of the information contained herein.

Trail Locations by Trail Number

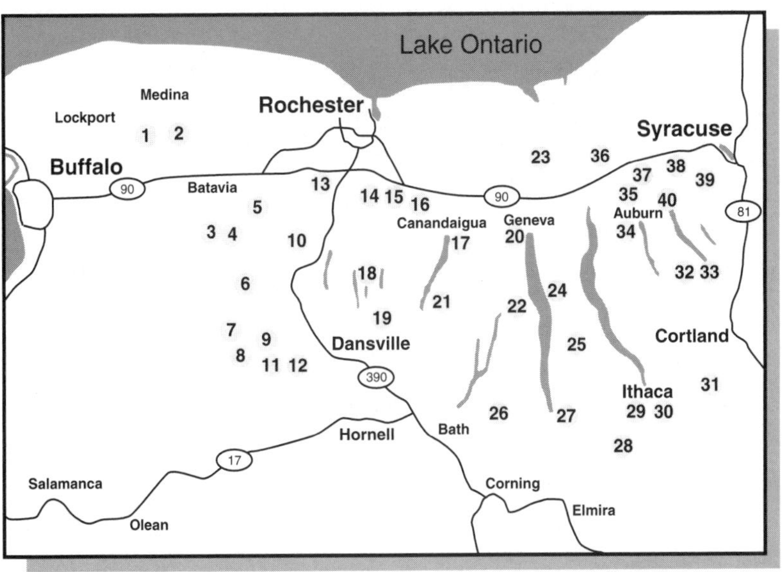

CONTENTS

Acknowledgments

The Finger Lakes and Genesee Valley Region is blessed with civic leaders and private citizens who have preserved our heritage and built the trails described in this book for all of us to enjoy. Through the preservation of abandoned railroad beds and the development of trails in woodland areas, they're gradually building a network of trails that will someday crisscross our area. Each year, more miles are opened as the land is secured, brush is cleared, and bridges are built to span the many waterways. The rides described by the maps and guides in this book are works in progress. Every year, more is accomplished by groups such as:

Erie Canal Park & Sims' Museum (David Beebe et al)
Friends of Genesee Valley Greenway (Fran Gotscik et al)
Friends of the Outlet (Phil Whitman et al)
Finger Lakes Trail Conference (Howard Beye, Chuck McLellan, Irene Szabo et al)
The Mendon Foundation (Carl Foss et al)
Ontario Pathways (Betsy Russell et al)
Victor Hiking Trails (Dave Wright et al)

We owe a debt of gratitude to these volunteer organizations. Without their hard work and dedication, we wouldn't have trails on which to ride or walk. We also thank the leaders of these groups for lending their time and energy to assure that the descriptions and facts about their trails are correct in this book.

Similarly, the foresight, planning, and action of our public officials has resulted in the paths dedicated to us bicyclists and outdoors enthusiasts. Kudos and thanks go to:

Casey Park (Bethany Walawonder et al)
Cayuga County Park and Trails Commission (Michelle Beilman et al)
Cayuga County Planning Board (Tom Higgins et al)
City of Rochester, Water and Lighting Bureau (Don Root et al)
Cornell Plantations
Finger Lakes National Forest Ranger District (Martha Twarkins et al)
Geneva Area Chamber of Commerce (Ben Wolf et al)

Genesee County Park & Forest (John Volpe et al)
Genesee County Planning (Joe Mancuso et al)
Iroquois National Wildlife Refuge (Dorothy Gerhart et al)
Letchworth State Park (Jayne McLaughlin, Rich Parker, et al)
New York State Department of Environmental Conservation (Jim Carpenter, David Conley, Jim Eckler, Greg Fuerst, John Hauber, Mark Keister, William Meehan, Jim Peek, Bruce Penrod, Ron Schroder, Wesley Stiles, Jack Watson, et al)
N.Y.S. Office of Parks, Recreation, & Historic Preservation (Chris Nielsen et al)
Perry Development Committee (E.D. Anna et al)
Sampson State Park
Seneca Lake State Park (Stephen Garlick et al)
Town of Dryden (James Schug et al)
Town of Ithaca Highway/Parks Department (Fred Noteboom et al)
Town of Jordan
Town of Skaneateles (Janet Aaron, Helen Ionta, et al)
Wayne County Planning Department (Jim Coulombe et al)

These people directed us to choice trails, reviewed our maps and descriptions, supplied historical tidbits, and often are responsible for the existence and maintenance of the trails. They have our sincere appreciation.

Introduction

"When the glaciers came they left in their wake a realm of gentle hills. And when the sun rose for the first time upon the new land, a spirit of the earth saw it and thought it so beautiful that he laid his hands upon the ground to bless it. When his hands were moved, the hollows left by his fingers were filled with water."

A local legend provided by the Finger Lakes Interpretive Center

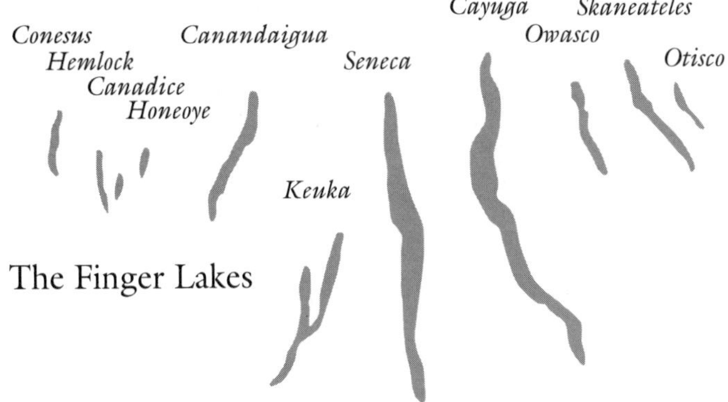

If you walk into a bike shop and ask where you can go bike riding and be safely off roads, you're not likely to hear many options. But, many trails are available in the Finger Lakes and Genesee Valley area; they're just a well kept secret. Well, the secret's out! This book is loaded with havens to which you can retreat for a short respite or a long adventure. Choose the length and type of terrain to fit the ability of the participants.

We enjoy bike riding very much. It makes us feel great, it's fun, and it's inexpensive. What a combination! But, we don't particularly like riding the narrow shoulder of a busy road as cars and trucks zip by within inches of our bikes. That's not relaxing and certainly not fun. Biking doesn't have to be like that. Off-road alternatives exist that are much more conducive to a family outing or an invigorating adventure. You'll find them in this book.

The American Heart Association recommends 30 to 60 minutes of physical activity at least 3 to 4 times per week to maintain cardiovascular fitness. You're more likely to achieve this level if you choose activities that you enjoy and that are convenient. Biking is a perfect way to improve the fitness of your heart and lungs. It burns calories too. Here's a breakdown of approximate calorie use per hour for three weight categories:

Person's Weight, lb.	Bicycling Rate, mph	Calories Burned per Hour
100	6	160
	12	270
150	6	240
	12	410
200	6	312
	12	534

You don't need a special (translation – expensive) bike to enjoy these trails. The only bike that isn't suited to an off-road venture is a road-racing bike. See the section "Types of Bikes" for specifics. The important thing is to grab this guide, hop on your bike, and go for a ride.

And, why stop at bicycling? Many of the trails listed in this book are equally well suited to hiking, cross-country skiing, bird watching, in-line skating, and running. Enjoy them at various seasons and using various means of locomotion. Each visit can be a unique experience. CAUTION: If you venture onto the rural trails during the fall hunting season, be sure to wear bright colors so that hunters can spot you easily.

Many of the trails in this book were built by and are maintained by volunteer or community groups. They all welcome new members, especially anyone who is willing to help with the work. This is especially true of trails open to bicycles. We need to earn the right to ride on trails by participating in the development and particularly in the maintenance of trails. We encourage everyone to join a trail group and benefit from the camaraderie and service to your community. You do not need to be a member of the sponsoring group to enjoy any of the trails in this guide.

If you find inaccurate information or substantially different conditions (after all, things do change), please send a note detailing your findings to:

Footprint Press
P.O. Box 645
Fishers, NY 14453

or e-mail us through our web site:

http://www.footprintpress.com

How To Use This Book

The trails are clustered into six geographic areas, using county boundaries as groupings and working west to east:

Rides in Orleans, Genesee & Wyoming Counties
Rides in Livingston & Monroe Counties
Rides in Ontario County
Rides in Yates, Wayne & Seneca Counties
Rides in Schuyler & Tompkins Counties
Rides in Cayuga & Onondaga Counties

The trails range in length from a short 1 mile to 29 miles, with the average being about 7 miles. The trails are ranked by length in an index in the back of the book, so you can select ones to fit the endurance of your group. Half of the trails are loops. Converted railroad beds and trails that follow current or past canals generally are not loops. When you retrace the route, however, the return trip can often look quite different from your new perspective, even though you're covering the same ground. Alternatively, to add variety, there is always the option of riding one way on the trails and the other on the roads. Some of the trails can be joined to lengthen your ride, or the ride can be shorten by turning back at any point along the route or parking a car at one of the alternative parking areas listed.

The riding times given are approximate and assume a moderate pace of 6 to 7 miles per hour. You may travel faster or slower, so adjust the times accordingly. Also, adjust the times to include stops or breaks for resting, eating, observing nature, viewing historical artifacts, and the like. You can easily stretch a two-hour bike ride into an all-afternoon affair, if you take time to enjoy the adventure along the way.

We listed some of the amenities you'll find as you travel. After all, when you work hard on a bike ride, you deserve a treat. (You'll quickly find as you read this book that we're ice cream lovers.) We also indicate bike shops that are located near the trails in case you require emergency repairs. Some of the trails are conducive to weekend getaways, so we've listed available camping and nearby bed-and-breakfast accommodations.

Legend

At the beginning of each trail listing, you'll find a map and a description with the following information:

Location: The closest town or lake and the county the trail is in.

Directions: How to find the trailhead parking area from a major road or town.

Alternative Parking: Other parking locations with access to the trail. Use these if you want to shorten your ride by starting or stopping at a spot other than the designated endpoint.

Riding Time: The approximate time that it will take to bike the trail one way at a moderate pace of 6 to 7 miles per hour, adjusted for the difficulty of the terrain. Add to this "riding time," the amount of time you stop for breaks, sightseeing, or other fun adventures to arrive at the total time needed for any particular outing.

Length: The distance from start to finish of each trek one way.

Difficulty: A rating of the amount of elevation change and type of riding surface you can expect. Each trail is rated on a scale of one to four boots.

(1 boot) Generally flat, a paved or hard-packed riding surface.

(2 boots) Could be rolling hills, a gradual grade, or a softer riding surface, so you'll pump those pedals a little harder.

(3 boots) Definitely hilly but not necessarily steep. A more rugged riding surface.

(4 boots) Steep hills or a rough trail. You'll get an aerobic workout for sure.

Surface: The materials that make up the trail bed for the majority of the trail.

Trail Markings: Markings used to designate the trails in this book vary widely. Some trails are not marked at all but are cleared or worn paths that you can easily follow. As long as there aren't many intersecting, unmarked paths, you shouldn't lose your way. Other trails are well marked with either signs, blazes, or markers and sometimes a combination of all three. Trail markings are established by the official group that maintains the trail.

Signs – wooden or metal signs with instructions in words or pictures.

Blazes – painted markings on trees showing where the trail goes. Many blazes are rectangular and placed at eye level. Colors may be used to denote different trails. If a tree has twin blazes beside one another, you should proceed cautiously because the trail either turns or another trail intersects.

Sometimes you'll see a section of trees with painted markings that aren't neat geometric shapes. These are probably boundary markers or trees marked for logging. Trail blazes are generally distinct geometric shapes and are placed at eye level.

Markers – small plastic or metal geometric shapes (square, round, triangular) nailed to trees at eye level to show where the trail goes. They also may be colored to denote different trails.

It is likely that at some point you will lose the blazes or markers while following a trail. The first thing to do is stop and look around. See if you can spot a blaze or marker by looking in all directions, including behind you. If not, backtrack until you see a blaze or marker then proceed forward again, carefully following the markings.

Uses: Each trail has a series of icons depicting the activity or activities allowed on the trail. Jogging and snowshoeing are allowed on all the trails. The icons include:

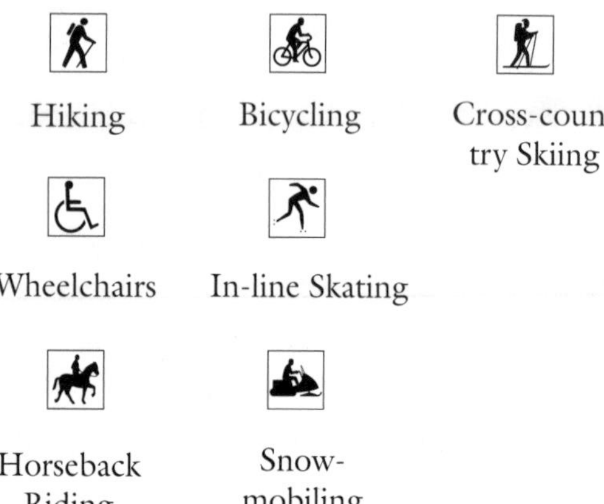

Contact: The address and phone number of the organization to call or write if you would like to join the organization, need additional information, or if you have any questions not answered in this book.

Map Legend

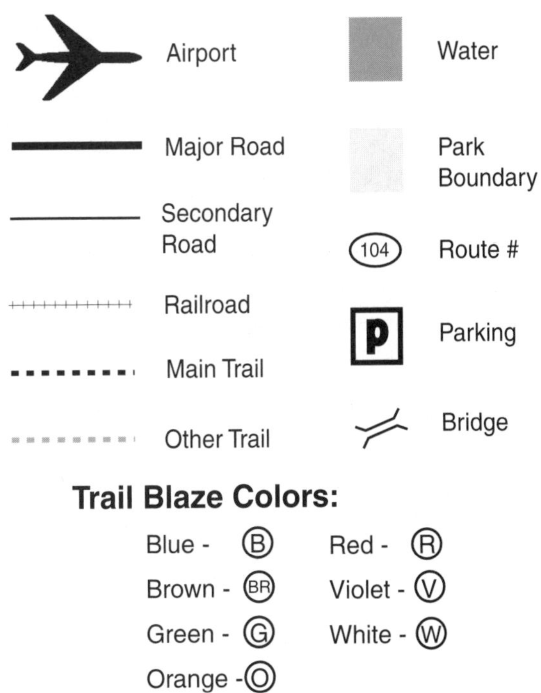

Directions

In the directions we often tell you to turn left or right. To avoid confusion in some instances we have noted a compass direction in parentheses according to the following:

(N) = north
(S) = south
(E) = east
(W) = west

Some trails have "Y" or "T" junctions. A "Y" junction indicates one path that turns into two paths. The direction we give is either bear left or bear right. A "T" junction is one path that ends at another. The direction is turn left or turn right.

Guidelines

Any adventure in the outdoors can be inherently dangerous. It's important to watch where you are going and keep an eye on children. Some of these trails are on private property where permission for passage is benevolently granted by the landowners. Please respect the landowners and their property. Follow all regulations posted on signs and stay on the trails. Our behavior today will determine how many of these wonderful trails remain for future generations to enjoy.

Follow "no-trace" ethics whenever you venture outdoors. "No-trace" ethics means that the only thing left behind as evidence of your passing are your footprints and tireprints. Carry out all trash you carry in. Do not litter. In fact, carry a plastic bag with you and pick up any litter you happen upon along the way. The trails included in this book are intended for day trips. Please, no camping or fires except in the few areas that identify camping is available under the "campgrounds" heading.

As the trails age and paths become worn, trail work groups sometimes reroute the trails. This helps control erosion and allows vegetation to return. It also means that if a sign or marker doesn't appear as it is described in the book, it's probably because of trail improvement.

Remember:
Take only pictures, leave only prints.
Please do not pick anything.

History of the Bicycle

For much of man's history on earth, he had two choices for getting around, either on foot or on the back of an animal (such as horses, mules, and wooly mammoths). Bicycles were developed to add another transportation option that multiplied human efficiency by a factor of approximately five. But the history of bicycles is very fuzzy. Sources often disagree as to the names of the inventors and the dates of their inventions. Leonardo DaVinci sketched a facsimile of the modern bicycle in 1490. It was way ahead of its time and, as far as we know, never left the drawing board. Around 1790 a French craftsman named de Sivrac developed a "Celerifere" running machine, which had two in-line wheels connected by a beam. The rider straddled the beam and propelled the Celerifere by pushing his feet on the ground, scooter fashion.

DaVinci's sketch

In 1817 German Baron Karl von Drais added steering. Several versions appeared around France and England by the early 1800s. As a replacement for the horse, these "hobby horses" became a short-lived craze. The roads of the time were too rutted to allow for efficient wheeled transport.

Celerifere

Scottish blacksmith Kirkpatrick MacMillan developed a rear-drive bike in 1839 using a treadle and rod for the rear drive mechanism. But, he lived in the Northern British Isles where people and ideas traveled slowly, so his invention didn't spread. R.W. Thompson patented a pneumatic tube in 1845. Prior to this invention, bikes had metal wheels.

The French anointed Ernest Michaux "father of the bicycle," as he and his brother Pierre added cranks and pedals. Their Velocipede started a bicycle boom. The larger front wheel made it faster but less stable. The war of 1812 brought an end to the French bicycle boom.

Velocipede

British engineers were next to pick up the design and improve upon it by adding ball bearings, pneumatic (Dunlop) tires, wire-spoked wheels, chain drive, variable gears, and cable controls. Over a twenty-year span, the British brought the bicycle to its present form, thanks mainly to James Starley of the Coventry Sewing Machine Company. In 1885 the Starley Rover safety bike was born, returning wheels to a reasonable size and improving the bike's stability.

Safety Bicycle

In the early days, women's dress (corsets, pointed shoes, and voluminous skirts) limited their participation in this new sport. Newspapers of the day railed against the "sorcers" or bicycle speedsters.

Types of Bikes

If you've shopped for a bicycle within the last ten years or so, you know that the choice can be overwhelming. So many types of bikes are available with unfamiliar names like derailleur, cruisers, mountain bikes, BMX, adult ballooners, and coaster-brake bikes. Gear speeds range from 1 to 21 speeds. To ride the trails listed in this book, you don't have to be an expert on bikes or have a specific type of bike. Many of the bikes housed in garages today (and often found at garage sales) are quire suitable on these trails. Let's review the major groups:

10-Speed Bikes

Derailleur bikes are commonly called 10-speed bikes, but they come in 5, 6, 10, 12, 15, or 20 speeds. The derailleur, a French word meaning "to derail," either lifts or pushes the chain from one gear to the next. These bikes are generally lightweight, with drop handlebars, hand brakes, no fenders, a narrow saddle, and high pressure tires. Designed to be racing bikes and long-distance pavement bikes, their popularity boomed in the 1970s. Derailleur bikes can be used on any of the paved trails in this book; they are not suited to the non-paved trails.

Single-Speed, Coaster-Brake Bikes

Baby boomers like us have grown up with these bikes. They are heavy bikes with low-pressure balloon tires, wide upright handlebars, a large padded seat, and as the name implies, only one speed. Braking is accomplished by backpedaling. Tough, sturdy work-horses, these bikes last a long time and can take a pounding on the trails listed in this book. Because of the single speed, you may occasionally find yourself walking up a hill. (But we do that anyway even with our 15-speed bikes!)

Cruisers or Adult Ballooners

Internal-hub-geared bikes or cruisers have many features in common with the single-speed, coaster-brake bikes except that they do have gear shifting. The shifting mechanism is contained inside the rear hub and is activated by hand brakes and cables from the handlebars. They come in 2, 3, or 5 speeds. The term "ballooners" derives from their fat, low-pressure tires. They make excellent trail bikes.

BMX Bikes

BMX is an abbreviation for Bicycle Moto-Cross. These tough bikes are mini-ballooners with fat tires originally designed for trick riding both on and off road.

Mountain Bikes

Mountain bikes also called all-terrain bikes (ATB), became the rage of the 1990s. They offer the functionality of a 10-speed bike, with the durability of a cruiser. Mountain bikes typically have flat handlebars; heavy-duty brake levers; indexed, thumb-shift levers; wide, knobby tires; heavy-duty rims; and reinforced frames. They're designed to be light weight and strong, as an all-terrain vehicle. Mountain bikes are available in 10, 15, 18, and 21 speeds.

Safety

Regardless of age, everyone who hops on a bike should wear an approved, protective helmet. It's the law in New York State for anyone under the age of 14. Wearing a bicycle helmet significantly reduces the chances of a serious brain injury if you fall off of your bike. Unfortunately, every year nearly 50,000 bicyclists suffer serious head injuries. Many never fully recover, and often the injuries are fatal. Why take the risk when prevention is so simple?

The best defense against a bicycle accident is the safe and skillful handling of the bicycle. But, some accidents are unavoidable, especially on trails where rocks, slippery roots, and woodchuck holes can present obstacles. Wearing a helmet while bicycling makes good sense. In the event of a fall, the helmet bears much of the impact and protects your skull and brain from the trauma that could result in serious injury or even death.

Three organizations have developed standards and test helmets to assure that they are effective in preventing head trauma. When selecting a helmet, look for a label or tag saying that the helmet meets the standards of ANSI (American National Standards Institute), ASTM (American Society of Testing and Materials), or Snell (Snell Memorial Foundation).

It's important that the helmet fits properly. It should sit level, cover your forehead, and not slide backward. Helmets come in many sizes; select one that feels comfortable and doesn't pinch. Then, use the sizing pads supplied with the helmet for "fine tuning" to achieve a snug fit. Finally, adjust the straps so that they are snug but not pinching. Now you're ready for an enjoyable and safe ride.

Courteous biking can help ensure that trails stay open for bikers. When you're around others, ride to the right in single file. Always signal before passing. It's easy for a bicycle to quickly sneak up on a pedestrian or slower biker and startle them. To avoid this, call out as you approach someone. A simple "on your left" alerts the person to your presence and lets them know which side you're approaching from. Ringing a bicycle bell has the same effect.

When you stop, pull off to the side of the path. Be conscious not to impede the progress of others. Stay on the trails. Do not create or use shortcuts, because they can result in added erosion to the area.

Bicycling with Children

Children love the excitement of bike riding. Add to that love new surroundings to explore, and you're sure to have a fun-filled adventure. Ensure a pleasant trip with these simple tips. Plan to take frequent breaks. Carry lots of water and some snacks. Play a game along the way. Read ahead in this guide and assign your child the task of finding the next area of interest. Let your child pick the next break spot. Take time to stop, point out, and discuss things you find on the trail, such as beaver dams, animal tracks, and flowers.

You may have noticed that it's hard to find helmets small enough for an infant. There's a good reason for that. Infants under 12 months of age should not, and can not legally ride in a bicycle child seat, trailer, sidecar, or any other carrier. The fact is that babies are so susceptible to brain injuries that the risks outweigh the rewards. More than a third of the injuries to babies in carriers occur when the bicycle falls over while standing still. So, please wait until your child is a year old before taking him or her along on this enjoyable sport.

Once your child passes the one-year mark, you can begin using a child seat that mounts on the bike's rear wheel. Make sure that the child is wearing an approved helmet and is securely but comfortably belted. The bicycle should have spoke protectors to assure that the child's feet stay out of harm's way. The child seat should be high enough to support the child's head. Remember, when transporting a child in a child seat, your bicycle will require a longer breaking distance, will be less maneuverable, and will swerve if the child shifts suddenly.

Dogs Welcome!

Outings with dogs can be fun with their keen sense of smell and different perspective on the world. Many times they find things that we would have passed without noticing. They're inquisitive about everything and make excellent companions. But to ensure that your "outing companion" enjoys the time outside, you must control your dog. Dogs are required to be leashed on most maintained public trails. The reasons are numerous, but the top ones are to protect dogs, to protect other hikers, and to ensure that your pet doesn't chase wildlife. Good dog manners go a long way toward creating goodwill and improving tolerance to their presence.

All of the trails listed in this book welcome dogs. Please respect the requirement that dogs be leashed where noted.

Clothing and Equipment

You don't need much more than a sturdy bicycle and a helmet to enjoy these trails. But here are some tips about clothing to wear and miscellaneous equipment to bring along. Shoes that tie or buckle are best; slip-on shoes could slip off unless they fit snugly. Sandals are not recommended. Sneakers are a good choice.

Dress in layers so you can peel down as your heart rate rises during the trip. You'll probably have to put the layers back on when you stop for a break. We find it convenient to have a handle-bar bag on the front of our bikes for discarded clothing and other items.

The one accessory that's mandatory is a bottle of water. It's easy to put a bottle holder on your bike or toss a water bottle in a handle-bar bag. Keeping hydrated is important even on a short trip.

Other handy things to have are an energy snack, a tire patch kit and pump, a first-aid kit, a bike lock, insect repellent, sunscreen, a hat, a raincoat, and this guidebook.

Bike Racks

The first challenge in being able to enjoy the trails listed in this book is getting your bicycle to the trailheads. This often requires some sort of bike rack. Bike racks come in many varieties and many prices. You can spend well over $200 or pick up one inexpensively at a garage sale. Before you head out shopping, think about the following questions to help you select a rack to fit your needs.

1. What vehicle will be used to reach the trailheads?
2. How many bikes will you need to transport?
3. Do the bikes all have quick-release front wheels?
4. Are any of the bikes an unusual size or shape (for example a small child's bike)?
5. Who will load the bicycles on the rack? Are they strong enough to lift the bicycles to the roof?
6. Will you need the extra security of a lockable bike rack?
7. Will the rack be specifically for bikes or do you also need to carry skis or other sports equipment?
8. How often are you likely to use the rack?
9. How much do you want to spend?

No rack is ideal for all vehicles and users. The tradeoffs you make will depend on your situation. For instance, if you plan to use the rack infrequently, you may be willing to tradeoff some ease-of-use for a lower price. Here's some of the variety you'll find as you shop:

- Roof racks attach to the top of a vehicle. It's important to know if your vehicle has gutters or not. Roof racks can be noisy from wind resistance. They require someone with strength to hoist the bicycles to the roof. You have to be careful not to forget that the bicycles are up there and drive into a garage. (We know this from experience!) With some roof racks, you can't open your vehicle's sun roof, however, they do allow full access to your trunk.
- Rear racks mount on the back of a vehicle with brackets and straps. They can scratch paint and can be hard to attach. Most limit your access to the trunk, but they are generally inexpensive, and you can load bikes quite easily.
- Hitch racks mount on the rear of a vehicle but use a trailer hitch as their main point of attachment. They're less likely to scratch your vehicle but are more expensive.
- Sport trailers are good for carrying many bicycles, but remember that you'll pay extra if you drive on a toll road. These trailers obviously require more storage space.

Rides in Orleans, Genesee, & Wyoming Counties

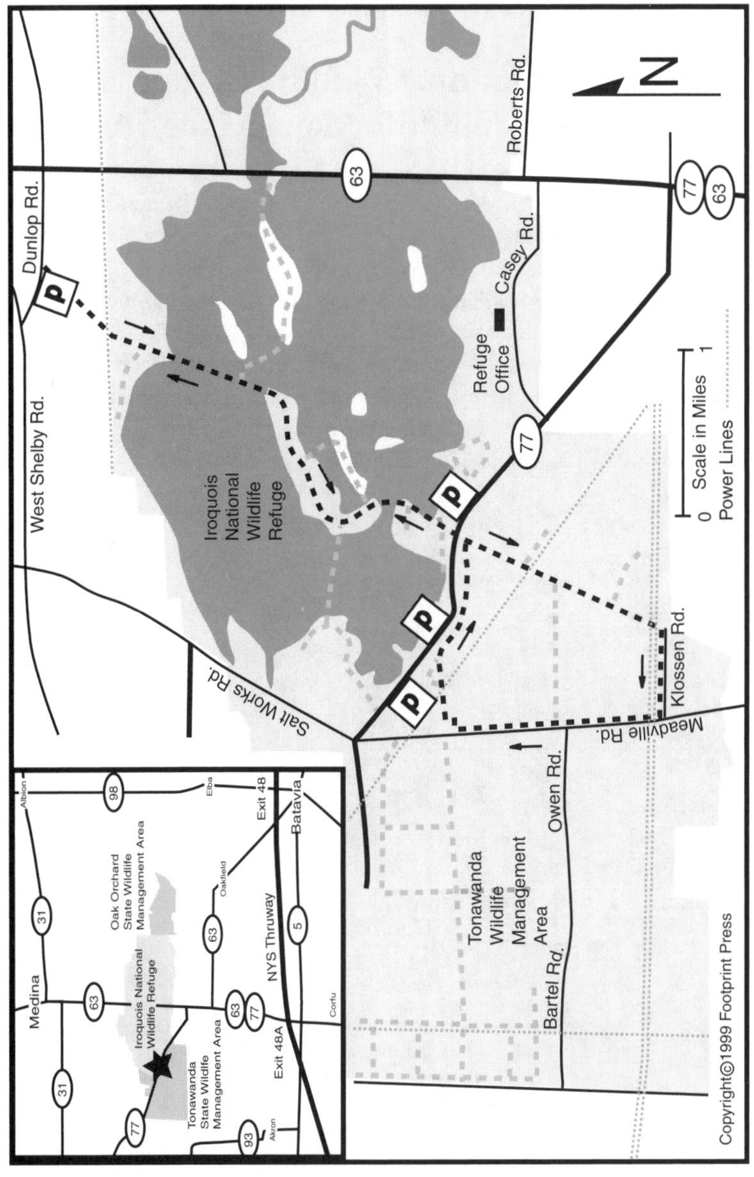

Iroquois National Wildlife Refuge and Tonawanda Wildlife Management Area

1.

Iroquois National Wildlife Refuge and Tonawanda Wildlife Management Area

Location: Iroquois National Wildlife Refuge and Tonawanda Wildlife Management Area, Alabama (northwest of Batavia), Genesee & Orleans Counties

Directions: The parking area is on the north side of Route 77 (Lewiston Road) between Casey Road and Salt Works Road. It's marked with a large brown and white sign for "Kanyoo Trail" and has brown and white maintenance buildings at the back of the parking lot.

Alternative Parking: The parking area on Dunlop Road, east of West Shelby Road

Hiking Time: 6.5 hours

Biking Time: 2 hours

Length: 12.5 mile loop

Difficulty:

Surface: Dirt, gravel, and packed grass tire tracks from State vehicles

Trail Markings: None

Uses: 

Dogs: OK on leash

Admission: Free

Contact: Iroquois National Wildlife Refuge
1101 Casey Road
Bascom, NY 14013
(716) 948-5445

N.Y.S. Department of Environmental Conservation
6274 E. Avon-Lima Road
Avon, NY 14414
(716) 226-2466
http://www.dec.state.ny.us

Iroquois National Wildlife Refuge and Tonawanda Wildlife Management Area join together with Oak Orchard Wildlife Management Area to form a total of 19,000 acres of impounded marshlands for the nurturing of wildlife.

Wildlife abounds on this trail, which in a previous era was called Feeder Road. On our trip, for example, deer watched from ahead on the path as we approached. Deciding we weren't natives, they leaped for cover with white tails flying. Great blue herons flew overhead, spreading large wings, and squawking their displeasure at us. White egrets spied us from treetops as they fished in open pools.

Along the way you'll pass intersections with a ski trail several times. This is a 7.5-mile loop around Mohawk Pool that is open for cross-country skiing in the winter. The ski trail is managed for wildlife nesting during summer months and is not available for hiking or biking. Other trails, dikes, and service roads in the area are also off limits to bicycles.

The Kanyoo Trail is a 1-mile loop hiking trail that is described in the book *Take A Hike! Family Walks in the Finger Lakes & Genesee Valley Region.*

Trail Directions

- From Kanyoo parking area turn right (N) on Route 77 (Lewiston Road).
- Cross Lewiston Road and in 0.1 mile, turn left (W) onto the gravel trail, after a guardrail. This is the south end of Feeder Road.
- Ride straight past a brown metal gate. A canal is on the left.
- At 0.7 mile, pass under power lines and pass a trail to the left.
- Pass a trail to the right.
- At 1.3 mile, continue straight on the grass, past a trail to the left.
- Reach power lines and a gravel road at 1.6 mile. Turn right (W) on Klossen Road and ride between the two sets of power lines.
- The road reaches a "T" at 2.2 miles. Turn right (N) on pavement.
- Pass houses.
- Pass Owen Road to the left.
- Pass a gravel trail to the right.
- Pass a path to the right with a barrier and stop sign.
- At 3.5 miles, immediately before a bridge over a canal with yellow and black stripped signs, turn right onto a dike and pass a barrier.
- At the top of the dike, turn left and follow the dike on packed grass.
- Pass under power lines at 3.9 miles.

- Pass a trail to the left. Continue as the trail bears right, parallel to Route 77.
- At 4.9 miles, reach a "T" and turn left (E) on a gravel trail. Pass a metal barricade and cross Route 77. (You can return to the parking lot at this point if you prefer a shorter ride.)
- Pass another barricade across Route 77, then pass a trail to the left. The trail is now a wide gravel lane – what used to be Feeder Road.
- Pass a trail to the right with a yellow metal barrier. This is the ski trail.
- The gravel lane (Feeder Road) bends left. A dike heads off to the left, then the gravel lane bends right.
- At 5.6 miles, the ski trail heads off to the right. Stay on old Feeder Road.
- Enter a wooded area.
- At 5.9 miles, pass a service road into the woods on your left.
- Pass the ski trail to the right again at 6.3 miles.
- Enter a field area (riding east) with Oneida Pool to your right.
- Pass a brown house on the left at 6.8 miles.
- Reach a junction with the ski trail to the right across the feeder canal. Continue straight (N).
- The feeder canal disappears into the woods to your right.
- Continue straight past a grass dike to the left.
- The trail bed turns to dirt as you enter the woods.
- Pass an old beaver dam in the feeder canal on the right.
- At 8.1 miles, pass overhead power lines and the buried gas line.
- At 8.7 miles, ride past the yellow metal barrier to the parking area on Dunlop Road.
- Turn around and retrace your path.
- At 10.3 miles, pass the brown house again.
- At 11.5 miles, pass the service road to the right with a brown sign "official vehicles only."
- Continue following the gravel path back to Route 77.
- Turn left to return to Kanyoo parking area.

Date Bicycled: ______________

Notes:

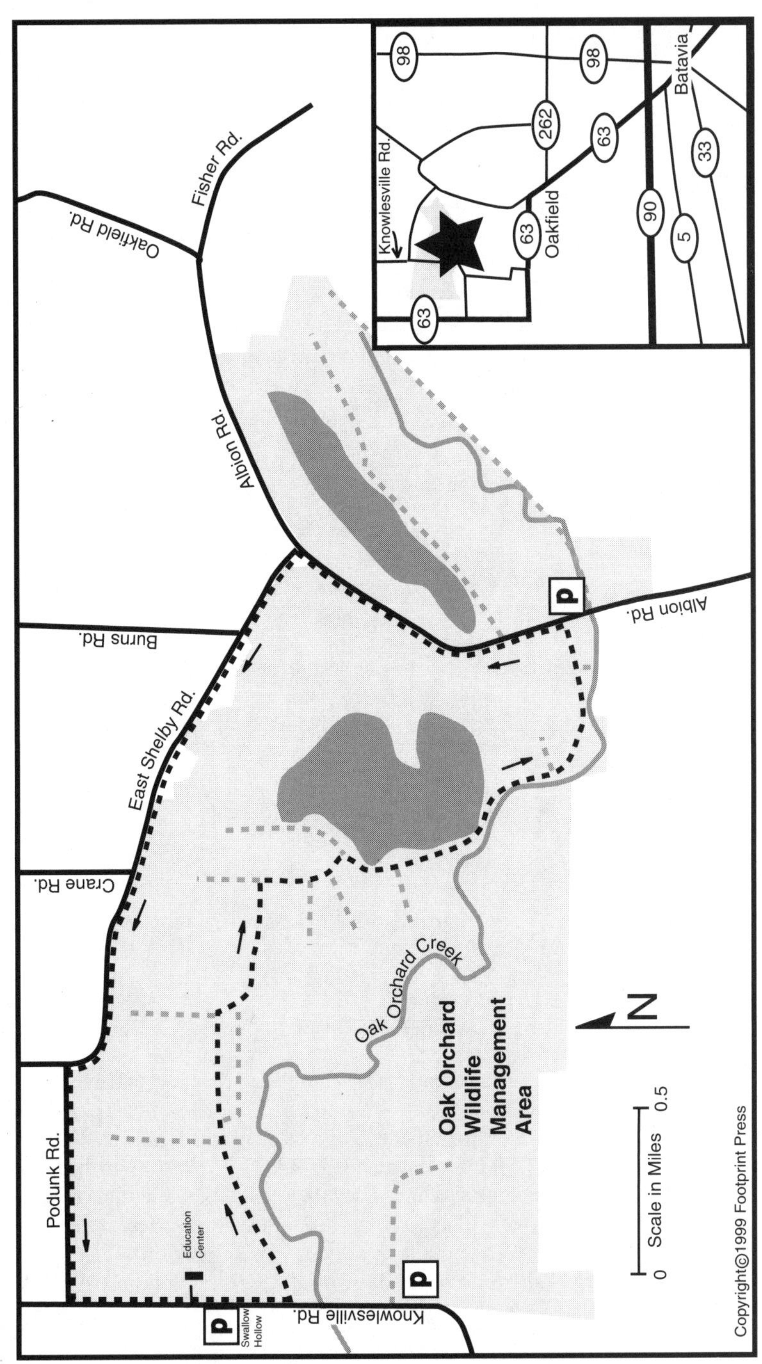

Oak Orchard Wildlife Management Area

2.
Oak Orchard Wildlife Management Area

Location:	Oak Orchard Wildlife Refuge, Alabama (northwest of Batavia), Genesee County
Directions:	From Batavia, follow Route 63 north. Turn east on Roberts Road and north on Knowlesville Road. The parking area, on the west side of Knowlesville Road, is marked with a large sign for "Swallow Hollow."
Alternative Parking:	The parking area on Albion Road, north of Oak Orchard Creek
Hiking Time:	4 hours
Biking Time:	1.25 hour
Length:	7.8 mile loop
Difficulty:	(1 boot if you go out and return on the dikes)
Surface:	Dirt, gravel, and packed grass tire tracks left by State vehicles
Trail Markings:	None
Uses:	  
Dogs:	OK on leash
Admission:	Free
Contact:	N.Y.S. Department of Environmental Conservation 6274 E. Avon-Lima Road Avon, NY 14414 (716) 226-2466 http://www.dec.state.ny.us

Oak Orchard Wildlife Management Area is the easternmost of three adjacent wildlife areas that cover a total of 19,000 acres. The other two areas are Tonawanda Wildlife Management Area and Iroquois National Wildlife Refuge. Oak Orchard Wildlife Management Area is located in an historic wetland known as "the Oak Orchard Swamp," created by a natural barrier across Oak Orchard Creek. This restriction is an outcropping of limestone located at Shelby Center that resisted the cutting action of the creek and created a huge wetland upstream. Historically, spring flooding of Oak

Windmill Marsh in Oak Orchard Wildlife Management Area.

Orchard Creek provided temporary water areas for migrating waterfowl, but by late spring, water levels would drop, leaving only a scant nesting habitat.

After the State acquired the land, wetland habitats were restored through the construction of perimeter dikes to create large impoundments of marsh vegetation. To provide the best possible habitat for wildlife, water levels in the impoundments are manipulated to create conditions that provide a mix of underwater plants, emergent vegetation, and open water.

Natural, undisturbed marshes thrive because of fluctuating water levels, which result from precipitation or lack of it. Periodic drying is important for the longevity of a marsh. During dry times the marsh soil is exposed to air, which allows it to consolidate, thus providing a good foothold for new plants. Dead organic matter decomposes and replenishes nutrients for growing plants. The dried soil provides an excellent bed for seed germination. To simulate this natural process, the Department of Environmental Conservation (D.E.C.) periodically drains areas of the marsh.

The primary objective for Oak Orchard Wildlife Management Area is to provide emergent marsh and grassland habitats for a variety of wildlife.

Riding the dike trails in Oak Orchard Wildlife Management Area.

Birding is best in the area from March through November, with peak waterfowl migrations occurring in mid-April and early October.

If you ride this area in summer, you'll notice a vivid carpet of purple flowers. Although pretty to look at, purple loosestrife is a detriment to the marshes. Purple loosestrife is not a native plant. In the 1800s seeds were brought to North America in the ballast holds of European ships. Since its introduction, it has spread rapidly across the continent. Once this plant gets a foothold, the habitat where fish and wildlife feed, seek shelter, reproduce, and rear young quickly becomes choked under a sea of purple flowers. Public and private groups across the continent have banded together in unparalleled cooperation to manage the purple loosestrife problem through education and eradication efforts.

The trails you'll ride are on the dikes around the marsh areas. The surface is dirt, gravel, and packed grass tire tracks from State vehicles. You may want to choose an overcast or cool day for your ride because there is no tree cover. Take along binoculars for spotting birds and other wildlife. We saw several deer along the way. Great blue herons would take off in front of us, spreading their large wings and trailing their long legs. Once a safe distance away, they'd squawk their displeasure at us. We even saw an eagle take flight across the marsh.

You have two options for this ride. Head out and back on the dikes for a total of 7 miles or head out on the dikes and return on the more hilly paved roads for a 7.8-mile loop.

Trail Directions

- Turn right (S) out of Swallow Hollow parking area onto Knowlesville Road.
- In 0.2 mile, turn left onto the trail, passing a yellow metal barricade.
- Pass a nest stand on the left. North Marsh Pond is also on your left.
- As you ride, you'll pass a series of small ponds on both sides of the dike. Some of these are potholes, dug as watering holes for the deer and other wildlife.
- Pass a trail to the left, then a water channel at 0.8 mile.
- Stay on the gravel tracks as they bend left, passing a trail to the right.
- At 1.1 miles stay on the trail as it bends right, passing a trail to the left.
- At the "T," turn right (S).
- At 1.4 miles the main trail bends left (SE) past a trail to the right.

- Pass a trail to the right. Water channels are now on both sides of the trail.
- Reach a "T" at 1.8 miles and turn right (S).
- Pass a trail to the right.
- Pass a trail to the left.
- At 2.3 miles, see the open water of Windmill Marsh Pond to the left.
- Pass a trail to the right and a water channel.
- Pass two old bridges across the channel to your right.
- The trail bends left over a culvert, with a small pond on the left.
- At 3.2 miles, the trail bends right (SE) through fields, with Oak Orchard Creek to your right.
- Pass around a brown metal gate to Route 9 (Fisher Road). You've come 3.5 miles. (You can turn around and retrace your path to the parking area from here or take the more hilly paved road option for 4.2 miles back to the parking area.)

To return via road:

- Turn left (N) onto County Route 9 (Albion Road).
- Turn left (NW) on East Shelby Road.
- Continue straight past Burns Road.
- Pass a trail to the left.
- At 5.7 miles, cross a bridge.
- Continue straight past Crane Road.
- Pass a trail to the left.
- At 6.4 miles, the road bends right, then left. Stay on the paved road.
- Reach the "T" of County Route 23 (Knowlesville Road) at 7.2 miles. Turn left (S).
- Only 0.5 mile left until the parking area at Swallow Hollow.

Date Bicycled: ____________

Notes:

Genesee County Park and Forest

Genesee County Park and Forest is the first and oldest county forest in New York State and owes its existence to Genesee County opening a home for the poor and a residence for the care and confinement of lunatics.

The poor were orphans, habitual drunkards, and paupers, including any person who was blind, lame, old, decrepit, or vagrant. Lunatics were described as persons who had understanding but by disease, grief, or other accident, had lost the use of reason. This classification also included anyone of unsound mind caused by old age, sickness, or weakness who was unable to manage his own affairs. Some of the old buildings can still be seen on the corner of Bethany Center Road and Raymond Road.

In 1882, the county purchased a wood lot to supply the cooking and heating needs of the "Poor House Farm" and sold wood for $0.75 a cord to cover expenses. In 1915, about 31,000 trees were planted at a cost of $225. These trees were the beginning of the establishment of the forest.

Riding the southern section on the Outer Loop in Genesee County Park and Forest.

More evergreens were planted in the 1920s, and 169,000 trees had been planted by 1935. The land was designated the first county forest in New York State.

Through the 1940s, 1950s, and 1960s, the county supervisors studied and discussed plans for a park. It wasn't until 1966 that funds were finally allocated. The Genesee County Park and Forest became a reality in 1971.

Today, this park is a gem rivaled by few others. Expanses of forest are interspersed with picnic areas, toboggan hills, horseshoe pits, volleyball courts, sandboxes, playgrounds, and baseball fields. Over the years, many volunteer groups have contributed to development of this park. In 1998, a group from Job Corps joined local volunteers to build a stunning nature center complete with stuffed animals and natural exhibits. Volunteers have begun offering a variety of nature programs on subjects ranging from turtles, to blue birds, to backyard composting. The nature center is open from 3:30 PM to 9:00 PM on weekdays and 9:00 AM to 9:00 PM on weekends.

The park is open daily from 9:00 AM until 9:00 PM. There is a unique Braille and large print nature trail near Raymond Road in Area A. This walking-only trail is bordered by a coated link railing so the blind can walk along the trail and read the Braille interpretive signs. Unfortunately, as is true throughout the park, some of the signs have been disturbed by vandalism. The county continually works on replacing signs in the park.

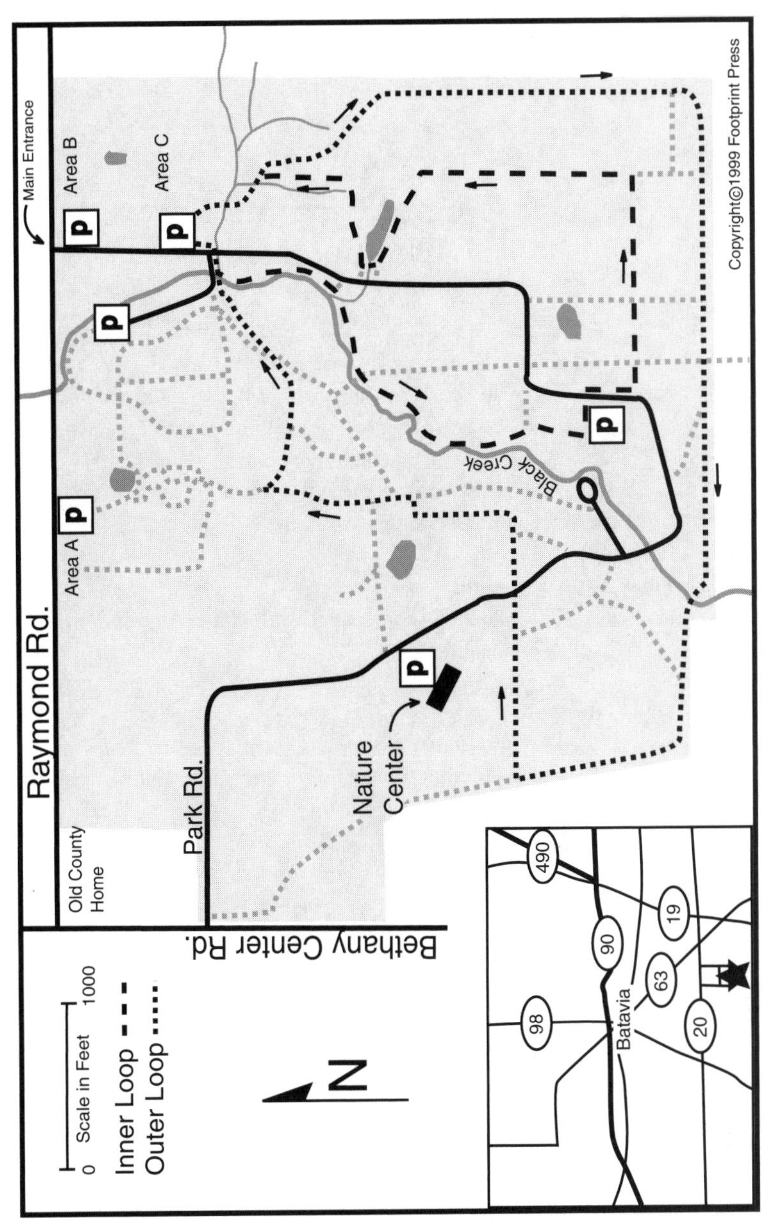

Genesee County Park and Forest

3.
Genesee County Park and Forest Outer Loop

Location: Bethany (south of Batavia, bordering the Wyoming County boundary), Genesee County

Directions: From Route 20, turn south on Bethany Center Road. Turn east on Raymond Road. Turn south off Raymond Road through the main park entrance onto Park Road. Park at the second parking area on the left (Area C).

Alternative Parking: The first parking area (Area B)

Hiking Time: 1.5 hour

Biking Time: 45 minutes

Length: 2.9 mile loop (combine with the inner loop trail for a 4.7-mile loop)

Difficulty:

Surface: Dirt and grass trails

Trail Markings: Some junction number signs and some trail name signs

Uses:  

Dogs: OK on leash

Admission: Free

Contact: Genesee County Park and Forest
11095 Bethany Center Road
East Bethany, NY 14054
(716) 344-1122

The outer loop trail is partially in the woods and partially through wide mowed swaths that can be warm when the sun is strong. It's challenging because of the hilly terrain and the mowed grass trails. This trail takes you into a less heavily used area of the park.

Bed and Breakfast: Roaring Creek Lodge B&B, 2761 West Main Street Road, Batavia, (716) 762-8881

Campgrounds: Lei-Ti Campground, 9979 Francis Road, Batavia, (800) 445-3484

Golden Mobile Campground, 5610 East Main Street Road, Batavia, (800) 528-9651

Trail Directions (designated by the short, dark, dashed lines on the map)

- From the second parking area (Area C), head south past a pavilion on the dirt trail.
- Bear left at the first junction and head uphill.
- Cross two small wooden bridges and continue uphill after each.
- Pass a small trail off to the right.
- At 0.8 mile, the trail turns right on a wide grass path. The trail will be a gradual downhill slope.
- Continue straight past two trails to the right.
- Continue straight through a trail intersection.
- At 1.2 miles, another trail will head off to the right. Continue straight, uphill.
- Cross two culverts, then pass a trail to the right.
- Climb a steep uphill grade. At the top of the hill, the trail bends right and then heads down. The trees to your right are Norway spruce.
- At 1.8 miles, turn right and head downhill on another grass trail. To your left is a forest of white cedar.
- Cross a small wooden bridge. The county plans to build a pond in the lowland to your right.
- Pass a trail to the right and continue uphill.
- At 2 miles, cross Park Road. Continue uphill on the grass path.
- Pass a woods trail on the right.
- At 2.2 miles, reach trail junction #6 (Wilderness Trail). Bear left on the Forestry Trail.
- Pass the second branch of the Wilderness Trail to the right. Stay on the Forestry Trail (green blazed).
- Soon, reach another junction and stay right on the Forestry Trail.
- The trail narrows, turns into dirt, and heads downhill through the woods.
- Turn right on the Conservation Trail (blue blazed) before a small wooden bridge.
- Enter a pine forest. Continue straight past a trail to the right.
- At 2.6 miles, continue straight (S) through junction #16.
- At 2.8 miles, turn right (SE) on a road. Cross a bridge over Black Creek. [To combine with the inner loop trail, turn right on the dirt trail after

the bridge.]
- Turn left at the stop sign onto Park Road.
- The parking area is a quick right.

Date Bicycled: ______________

Notes:

4.
Genesee County Park and Forest Inner Loop

Location: Bethany (south of Batavia bordering the Wyoming County boundary), Genesee County

Directions: Turn south off Raymond Road through the main park entrance onto Park Road. Park at the second parking area on the left (Area C).

Alternative Parking: The first parking area (Area B)

Hiking Time: 2 hours

Biking Time: 25 minutes

Length: 1.8 mile loop (combine with the outer loop trail for a 4.7 mile loop)

Difficulty:

Surface: Dirt and gravel trails with roots

Trail Markings: Some junction number signs and some tail name signs

Uses:  

Dogs: OK on leash

Admission: Free

Contact: Genesee County Park and Forest
11095 Bethany Center Road
East Bethany, NY 14054
(716) 344-1122

See the map on page 41. This inner loop trail takes you through hilly terrain in the woods. Sometimes you'll travel on narrow trails along Black Creek and sometimes on wide trails, but always shaded by a canopy of trees. Choose this route for a hot or sunny day. In addition to the hills, the challenge comes from riding over roots across the trail.

Bed and Breakfast: Roaring Creek Lodge B&B, 2761 West Main Street Road, Batavia, (716) 762-8881

Campgrounds: Lei-Ti Campground, 9979 Francis Road, Batavia, (800) 445-3484

Golden Mobile Campground, 5610 East Main Street Road, Batavia, (800) 528-9651

Trail Directions (designated by the long, dark dashed lines on the map)

- From the second parking area (Area C), head left (S) on Park Road.
- Take a quick right on the paved road.
- Immediately before the bridge, turn left onto the trail.
- Cross a cement bridge. This narrow gravel trail through the woods follows Black Creek.
- At the trail junction bear right and cross a boardwalk.
- Continue straight (SW) through a trail intersection. The terrain now gets hilly.
- Bear right at a "Y" junction and head uphill.
- At 0.7 mile, reach a parking area and turn left.
- Turn right onto Park Road.
- In 0.1 mile, take the first left (E), on a wide dirt trail, shaded by the woods.
- Continue straight through two intersections.
- At 1.1 miles, reach a "T" and turn left (N).
- The terrain continues to be hilly. Pass a swamp to the right.
- Turn right in front of the pavilion. (If you reach the road you rode too far.)
- Now a steep uphill to a "T." Turn right and continue uphill.
- The terrain will be hilly.
- Reach another "T." Turn left (NW).
  [To combine this loop with the outer loop, turn right at the "T."]
- Pass a pavilion and cross a creek to the parking lot.

Date Bicycled: ______________

Notes:

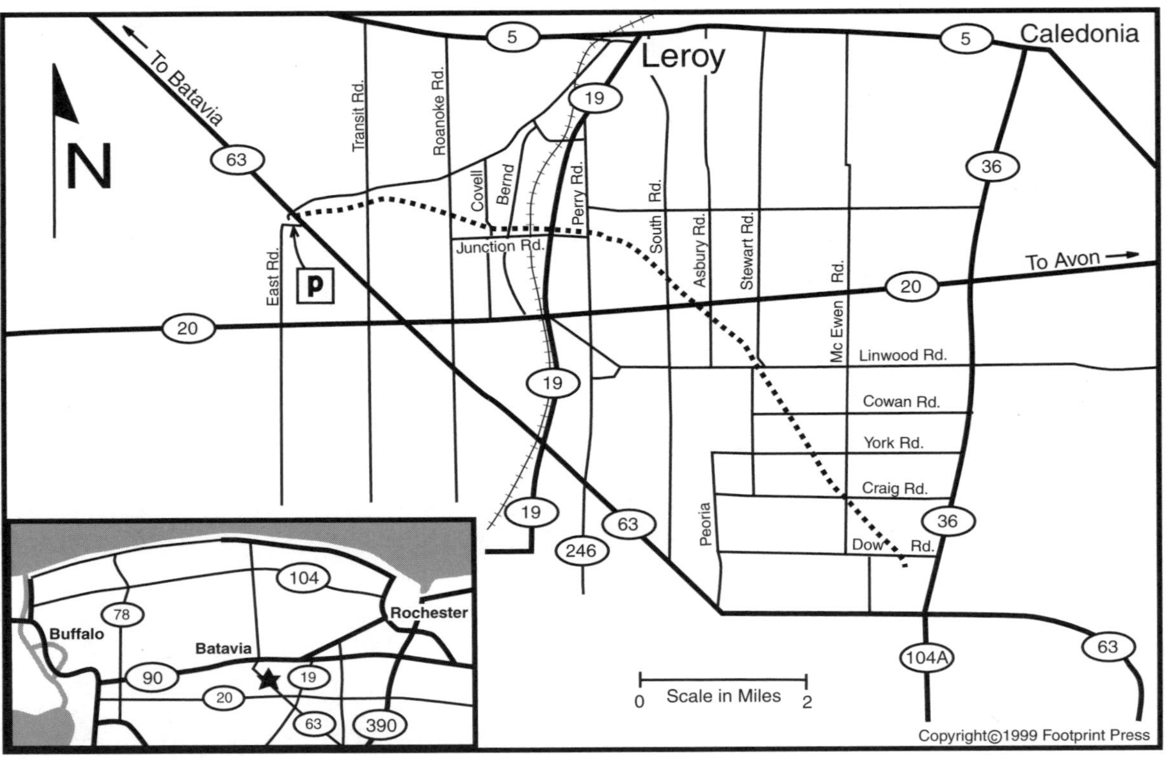

Groveland Secondary

5.
Groveland Secondary

Location: South of Leroy, Livingston and Genesee Counties

Directions: From Batavia, take Route 63 south. The trailhead is across from East Road. There is no official parking area. Park along the edge of East Road.

Alternative Parking: Along the roadside at most of the road crossings (Craig Road is the last road south where parking is available before the trail turns to ballast stone.)

Hiking Time: 7 hours

Biking Time: 2.25 hours

Length: 13.3 miles one way

Difficulty:

Surface: Mostly gravel, some ballast stone

Trail Markings: None

Uses:   

Dogs: OK on leash

Admission: Free

Contact: N.Y.S. Department of Environmental Conservation
6274 East Avon-Lima Road
Avon, NY 14414
(716) 226-2466

This former railroad bed was purchased from Consolidated Rail Corporation of Pennsylvania in 1991. It was known at that time as the Erie Lackawanna – Groveland Branch. All rails and ties, and most of the ballast were removed from the double line, but this trail continues to be a work in progress. The ballast is currently not cleared south of Dow Road.

Trail Directions

- Across Route 63, pass the yellow metal gate with a stop sign.
- At 0.5 mile, cross a mowed ATV path leading to private lands.
- Pass barriers on both sides of the road as you cross Transit Road at 1.3 miles.
- Cross Oatka Creek on a trestle bridge at 1.4 miles. Notice the other

The abandoned railbed of Groveland Secondary Trail.

railroad trestle 300 feet to the north.

- Pass several entrances to farm fields, then the backyard of a home.
- At 2.6 miles, cross Roanoke Road.
- Cross another branch of Oatka Creek.
- Cross Covell Road at 3.3 miles (roadside parking available).
- At 3.6 miles, cross Bernd Road (roadside parking available).
- Ride on ballast for 0.4 mile.
- Ride down then back up, across an active rail line (The Rochester Southern) at 4.0 miles.
- Cross Route 19 at 4.4 miles (roadside parking available).
- Pass a farm field access road.
- At 5.0 miles, cross Perry Road (roadside parking available).
- Cross a private access road (former Summit Road).
- At 6.7 miles, cross South Road (roadside parking available).
- Cross Route 20 at 7.4 miles.
- Cross Asbury Road at 7.6 miles (roadside parking available).
- At 9.0 miles, cross Stewart Road (roadside parking available at Stewart and Linwood).
- Cross Cowan Road (roadside parking available).
- At 10.8 miles, cross York Road.
- Cross a bridge.
- Cross Craig Road at 11.8 miles (roadside parking available).
- Cross the gas pipeline.
- At 13.3 miles, turn around and retrace your path. (Or, cross over Dow Road on an old bridge. Just beyond the bridge, ballast stone begins. The trail will continue south as the ballast is removed.)

Date Bicycled: ______________

Notes:

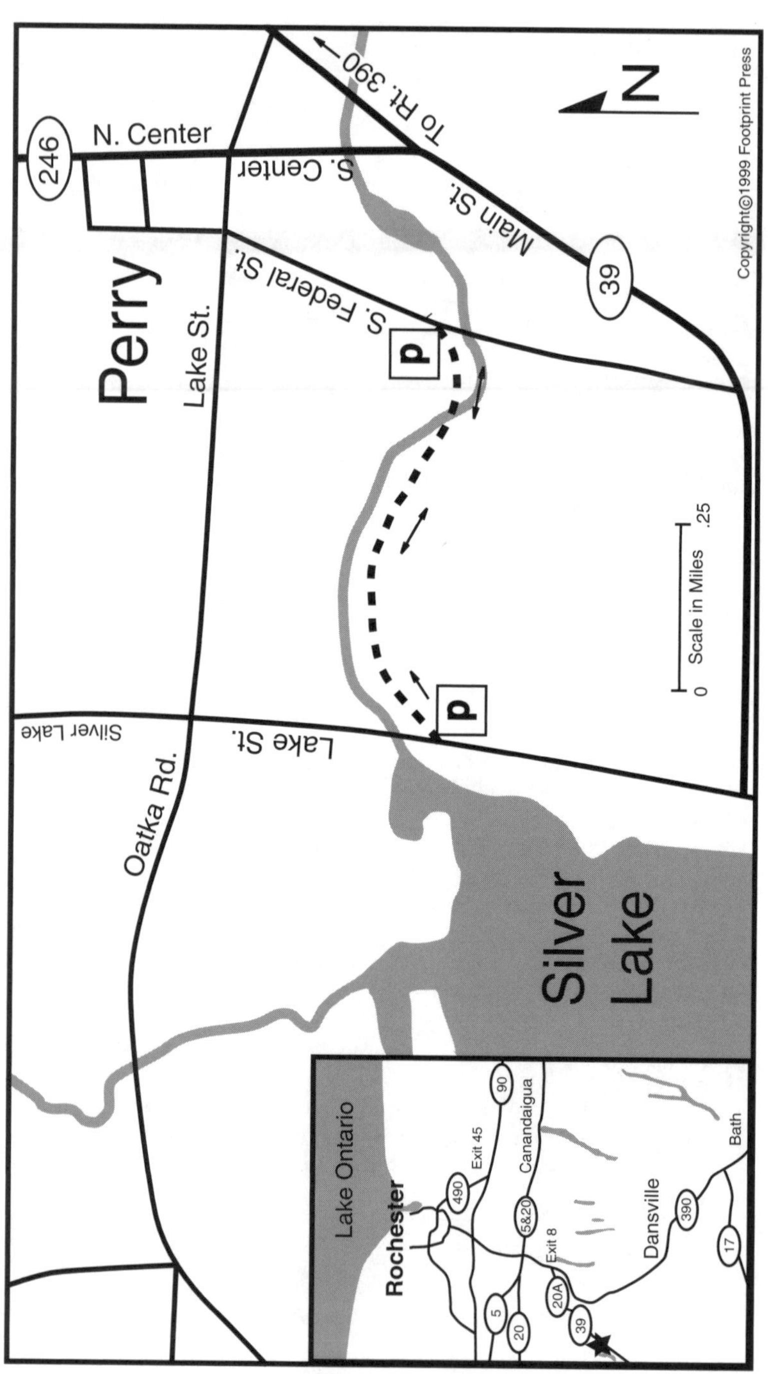

Silver Lake Outlet

6.
Silver Lake Outlet

Location: Perry (north end of Silver Lake), Wyoming County
Directions: Exit Route 390 at Geneseo (exit 8). Head west, passing though Geneseo, then turn west on Route 39. In the village of Perry, head west on Lake Street. Turn left to remain on Lake Street (continuing straight, the road turns into Oatka Road). Cross over the outlet. The parking area is a dirt road south of the outlet.
Alternative Parking: South Federal Street parking area
Hiking Time: 20 minutes
Biking Time: 10 minutes
Length: 0.8 mile round trip
Difficulty: 
Surface: Dirt trail
Trail Markings: None, but easy-to-follow
Uses: 
Dogs: OK on leash
Admission: Free
Contact: Perry Development Committee
25 South Main Street
Perry, NY 14530
(716) 237-4090

Silver Lake Outlet Trail is a short stroll or ride on a dirt path, which once was a railroad bed. A tree canopy will shade your way. In June, the trail is lined with forget-me-nots and wild strawberries. The Silver Lake Outlet is a slow-flowing stream but it is a favorite of people fishing. The waters are alive with Perch, Bullhead, Sunfish, Northern Pike, Bass, Crappie, and Walleye.

As you ride, keep your eyes peeled for the Silver Lake sea serpent. In 1855, a group of fisherman spotted what was first thought to be a floating log. But as it moved they changed their description to that of a monster with a serpentine body and horrid-looking head. Over the next several months, numerous people claimed sightings. Observation towers were built along the shore and were manned by men known to be of good character. Expeditions were mounted to capture the beast, including one by a professional whaler. Business boomed at Perry's hotels and restaurants. Over time the sightings died away and life settled back to normal in Perry. There was some evidence that the serpent was a hoax perpetrated by the owner of a large Perry hotel called the Walker House. But, townsfolk claim the sea serpent may just be hibernating, waiting for the right time to reappear.

Bed & Breakfast:	Perry Bed & Breakfast, 9 N. Federal Street, Perry, (716) 237-6289
Campgrounds:	Woodstream Campsite, 5440 School Road, Gainsville, (716) 493-5643
	Zintel & Norris Campsite, 156 Lakeshore Drive, Castile, (716) 237-3080
Bike Repair:	Grandpa's Bike Repair, 10 Tuna Street, Perry, (716) 237-2748

Trail Directions

- Follow the dirt road toward a metal barricade and the sign "Perry Welcomes You to Silver Lake Trail."
- The outlet will appear on your left.
- Cross a wooden bridge over the outlet.
- Reach a parking area off South Federal Street.
- Turn around and retrace your path.

  [Or, to follow roads back, turn left on South Federal Street and a left on Lake Street. Follow Lake Street as it turns left along the east side of Silver Lake to return to the parking area.]

Date Bicycled: ______________

Notes:

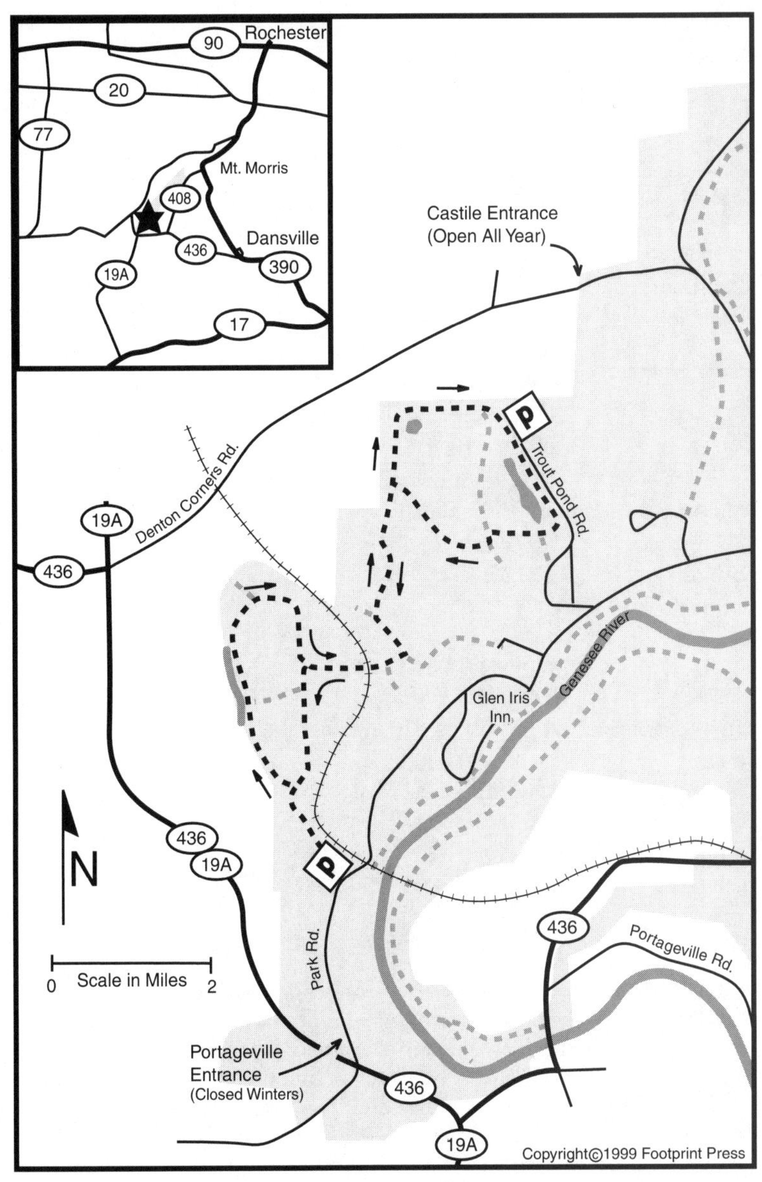

Letchworth State Park - Trout Pond Loop

7.
Letchworth State Park – Trout Pond Loop

Location:	Castile and Portageville, Wyoming County
Directions:	From Route 390, head south on Route 408 through Mount Morris. In Nunda, turn west on Route 436. Follow Route 436 over the Genesee River and through Portageville, turning right at the Portageville entrance to Letchworth State Park. The parking area will be on the left just before the large railroad trestle.
Alternative Parking:	At the end of Trout Pond Road
Biking Time:	1.75 hours
Length:	6.1 mile loop
Difficulty:	(mountain bike trail)
Surface:	Dirt trails
Trail Markings:	Yellow blazes with trail numbers inside
Uses:	
Dogs:	OK on leash
Admission:	$4 per vehicle park entrance fee
Contact:	Letchworth State Park Castile, NY 14427 (716) 493-3600

Letchworth State Park follows the banks of the Genesee River, which has cut deep cliffs over the past tens of millions of years and continues to do so each year. It contains three major waterfalls, one of which is over 107 feet high. In 1859, Mr. William Pryor Letchworth purchased the Glen Iris Inn building and surrounding 1,000 acres of land. He developed the Inn and grounds and then deeded his estate to the State of New York in 1907. Today, Glen Iris Inn is open for fine dining and overnight accommodations from Good Friday until New Year's Day. The William Pryor Letchworth Museum has been open since 1913. It displays Native American artifacts, early photographs of Mr. Letchworth's estate, and Mr. Letchworth's personal library.

Riding downhill toward Deh-Ga-Ya-Soh Creek.

Known for its Genesee River Gorge, the "Grand Canyon of the East" attracts many visitors each year. Most visitors don't venture far from their cars and miss much of the 14,350-acre park. That's why you're not likely to encounter many others as you pedal this back woods section of the park.

The Portage High Bridge, which is visible from the parking area, was originally built in 1852, using wood from 300 acres of forest. It burned in 1875 and was replaced with the structure you see today. It is still used daily to carry trains over the Genesee River Gorge.

This ride is best for hybrid or mountain bikes. The woods trails have roots and steep sections. You'll be riding trails 2, 2A, and 3. Letchworth State Park has 67 miles of hiking trails. Bicycles are allowed only on park roads and on trails 2, 2A, 3, 5, 7, 8, 8A, 10, 11,13, 19, and 20.

Campgrounds:	Four Winds Campground, 7350 Tenefly Road, Portageville, (716) 493-2794
	Letchworth State Park Highbanks Camping, (800) 456-2267

Lodging: Glen Iris Inn, 7 Letchworth State Park, Castile, (716) 493-2622

Trail Directions

- From the parking area, head uphill on the gravel trail, bearing left (W) at the first "Y." Follow yellow blazes with a number 2 inside.
- Reach the level of the railroad tracks and the trail bends left through the woods.
- Cross a raised culvert over De-Ge-Wa-Nus Creek.
- At 0.4 mile, reach a wide grass area. The wide trail bends right but you should continue straight (NW) uphill on a narrow trail. (The wide trail will be your return route.)
- A dammed waterway will appear on your left. Enter a pine woods and the trail will level out. Continue following yellow #2 blazes.
- Notice all the gnawed off trees from former beaver activity in the area.
- At 0.8 mile, there is a yellow blazed trail to the right. It's a green foot path, not a well-worn dirt trail, so you're likely to miss it. Continue following yellow #2 blazes along the waterway.
- At 1.0 mile, reach a mower turnaround and turn right onto a wide mowed trail.
- The trail bends right.
- Bear left (E) at a "Y."
- Pass a snowmobile trail sign pointing to Perry, Mt. Morris, and Trailside

Pausing for a brake to admire Deh-Ga-Ya-Soh Creek.

The railroad tunnel along Trout Pond Loop.

Lodge. Blazes are still yellow #2.

- Ride downhill then under the railroad tunnel. You've come 1.8 miles.
- Pass a trail on the right then quickly reach a "T." Turn left (NW) heading uphill on yellow #2A. (The yellow #2 blazes go right.)
- At the top of the hill turn right (E) at the yellow arrow. You've come 2 miles.
- A long, steep downhill will take you to a bridge crossing Deh-Ga-Ya-Soh Creek.
- Across the creek, head uphill, cross a second bridge, and continue up.
- Continue straight past a trail on the right. (It will be part of your return loop.)
- Circle around Pine Pond, still following yellow #2A blazes.
- Continue straight (E) on yellow #3, past a trail to the right (also yellow #3).
- Pass a grass trail on the left. Continue bending right on the dirt trail.
- At 3.4 miles, pass Trout Pond and picnic tables on the right.
- At the end of the pond, turn right (W) and cross the earthen dam to the yellow #3 trail.
- Pass a trail to the left, which goes to a park service area.
- Reach a "T" with a large yellow and brown trail map. Turn left (S) on

yellow #2A.

- Reach another "T" and turn right (W), staying on yellow #2A.
- At 4.2 miles, reach another "T." Turn left (S), heading downhill to a bridge.
- Continue downhill and across a second bridge.
- Reach a "T" and turn left.
- Quickly reach another "T" and turn right (W) on yellow #2. Pass a trail on the left.
- At 5.1 miles, ride through the railroad tunnel.
- Bear left at a "Y," staying on yellow #2. A snowmobile sign points to Portageville.
- Pass a trail to the right as you head downhill.
- At 5.6 miles, you'll reach a grassy area and a "T," turn left (S).
- Follow the trail back downhill to the parking area.

Date Bicycled: ____________

Notes:

Rides in Livingston & Monroe Counties

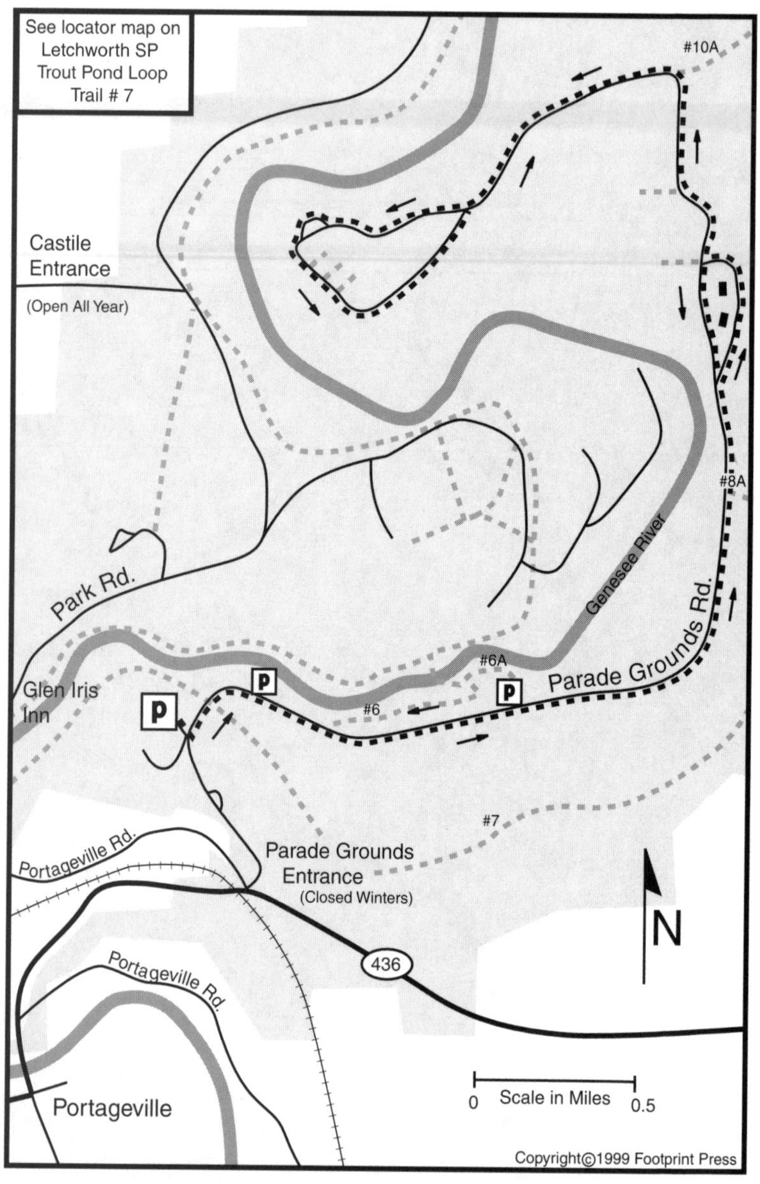

Letchworth State Park - Big Bend Loop

8.
Letchworth State Park – Big Bend Loop

Location:	South of Mount Morris, Livingston County
Directions:	From Route 390, head south on Route 408 through Mount Morris. In Nunda, turn west on Route 436. Shortly before the Genesee River, turn right into the Parade Grounds area. Pass a lookout loop on the right. The Parade Grounds parking area will be on the left.
Alternative Parking:	At the overlook on Parade Grounds Road At the intersection of trail 6A and the Parade Grounds Road
Biking Time:	1.5 hours
Length:	9.5 mile loop
Difficulty:	
Surface:	Paved and gravel roads
Trail Markings:	None
Uses:	 
Dogs:	OK on leash
Admission:	Free (entrance is free to the east side of the park)
Contact:	Letchworth State Park Castile, NY 14427 (716) 493-3600

This route begins at the Parade Grounds, an infantry parade grounds during the Civil War. It follows a lesser-used park road heading gradually uphill, then continues on old gravel roads, which are driveable but rough for cars. You'll ride out to the bend of the Genesee River, with views of the gorge cliffs where they're the highest. Parade Grounds Road is closed in the winter, making this route good for cross-country skiing.

At Big Bend, the Genesee River almost doubles over on itself. This twisting is unusual for such deep canyons. In its early days, more than 10,000 years ago, the Genesee River crossed a plateau. It was free to sidewind like a snake as it began to cut through the sandstone and shale. Once the

The cliffs of Letchworth Gorge.

winding course was set, the river dug its way down to create the 600 feet cliffs of today.

Bed & Breakfasts: Brown's Butternut B&B, 44 East Street, Nunda, (716) 468-2805

Highbridge Inn B&B, 203 Portageville Road, Portageville, (716) 468-2611

Campgrounds:	Four Winds Campground, 7350 Tenefly Road, Portageville, (716) 493-2794
	Letchworth State Park Highbanks Camping, (800) 456-2267
Lodging:	Glen Iris Inn, 7 Letchworth State Park, Castile, (716) 493-2622

Trail Directions

- From the Parade Grounds parking area, head left (NE) on the paved Parade Grounds Road.
- Pass an overlook on the left.
- Pass trail #6 on the left.
- At 1.0 mile, pass trail #6A and a parking area on the left. The road will get rougher and hillier.
- At 1.8 miles, the road turns to gravel then returns to a one lane paved road. Pass trail #8A on the left.
- At 2.3 miles, bear right at the "Y." (Left will be part of your return loop.)
- Pass cabins, outhouses, and trail #9 to the right.
- Turn right on the gravel road as the paved road bends left. Ride uphill.
- Pass a maintenance road on the left.
- Pass narrow grass trail #10A on the right.
- The road becomes two parallel tracks.
- At 4.4 miles, reach a lookout.
- Pass a maintenance trail and then several mowed paths on the left.
- At 5.2 miles, reach a road junction and continue straight.
- Pass trail #10A to the left.
- Reach pavement at 6.6 miles and continue straight.
- Pass the cabin loop road on the left.
- Pass trail #8A on the left.
- Pass trail #6A and parking on the right.
- Pass trail #6 on the right.
- Pass a swamp on the left.
- At 9.1 miles, pass the overlook and parking on the right.
- Pass the trail #7 intersection.
- Turn right into the Parade Grounds parking area.

Date Bicycled: ______________
Notes:

Genesee Valley Greenway

The Genesee Valley Greenway is a 90-mile historic and natural resource corridor that follows a transportation route that was once used by the Genesee Valley Canal, from 1840 to 1878, and later by the railroad, from 1880 to the mid 1960s. The former rail bed now serves as a multi-use trail open to hikers, bikers, horseback riders, cross-country skiers, and snowmobilers. Currently, 40 miles of the total 90 miles are open for use. Each year, more segments are opened.

Three segments are described in this book. The trail will eventually connect with the Rochester River Trail, the Erie Canalway Trail, the Finger Lakes Trail, the Lehigh Valley Trail, as well as Rochester's Genesee Valley Park and Letchworth State Park. The Genesee Valley Greenway passes through wetlands, woodlands, rolling farmlands, steep gorges, historic villages, and the Genesee and Black Creek valleys. It offers something for everyone, from a short ride to a challenging long-distance trek. You can stop to explore quaint villages, visit an historic canal era inn, or inspect well-preserved stone locks and other remnants of the ingenuity and engineering that built the canal and the railroad.

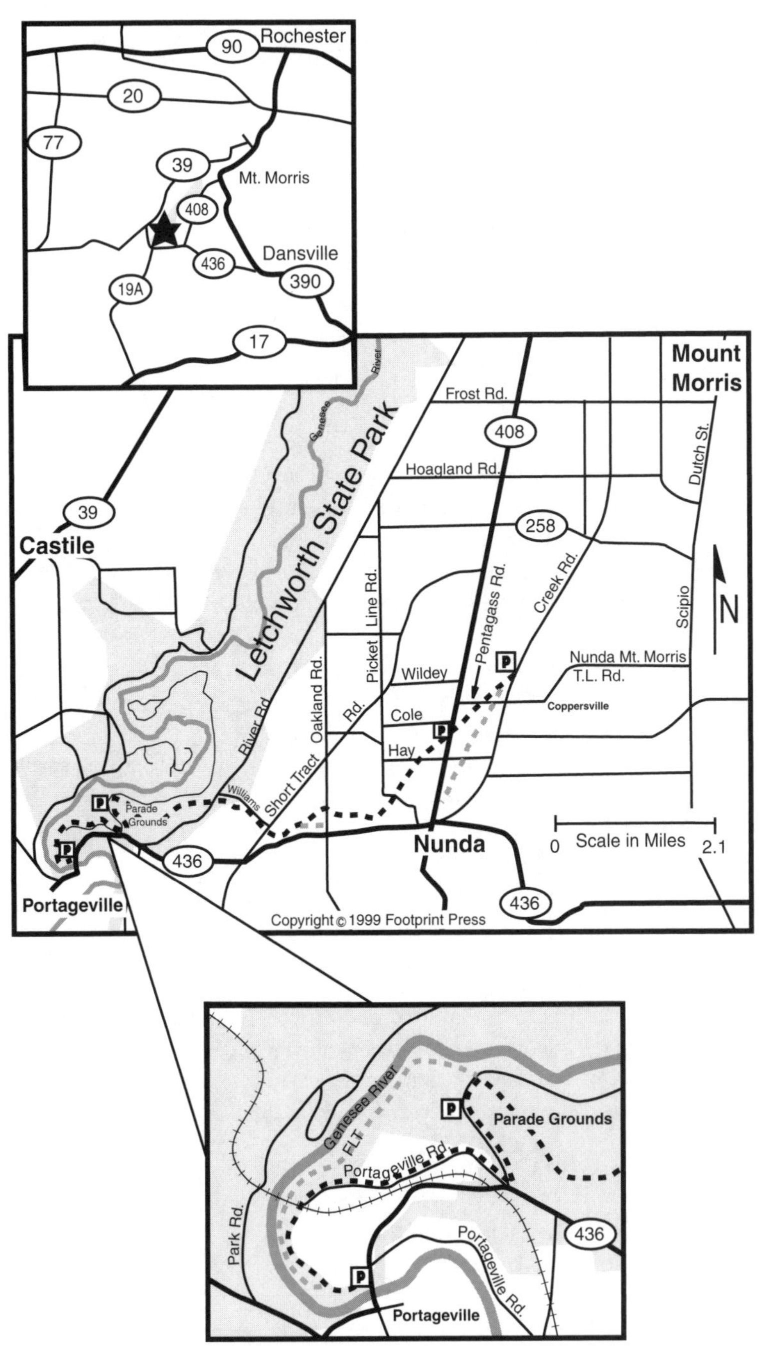

Genesee Valley Greenway - Portageville to Nunda

9.

Genesee Valley Greenway Portageville to Nunda

Location: Portageville to Nunda, Livingston County

Directions: From Route 390, head south on Route 408. In Nunda turn west on Route 436. Park off Highway 436 on the northern side of the Genesee River, just north of Portageville. The parking area has a "Finger Lakes Trail" sign, a large black-and-yellow pedestrian sign, and a "Road Closed" sign.

Alternative Parking: Parade Grounds (closed in winter): Turn north off Route 436 at the sign "Letchworth State Park Parade Grounds." Parking is on the left in the picnic and playground area. Restrooms are available. The trail is a short distance down the road.
Route 408
Creek Road just north of Coopersville (There is a small white sign set back from the road.)

Riding Time: 1.5 hours

Length: 9.5 miles one way

Difficulty: If you begin in Portageville
If you begin at Parade Grounds

Surface: Dirt trail, mowed grass, packed gravel, and paved road

Trail Markings: Sporadic yellow blazes; green "Genesee Valley Greenway" signs on the eastern portion. Yellow metal gates at road crossings from the Parade Grounds east.

Uses:
(The portion located in Letchworth State Park is open for biking from June 1 to October 1.)

Dogs: OK on leash

Admission: Free

Contact: Friends of the Genesee Valley Greenway, Inc.
P.O. Box 42
Mount Morris, NY 14510
(716) 658-2569
http://www.netacc.net/~fogvg

N.Y.S. Office of Parks, Recreation, and Historic Preservation
Western District - Genesee Region
One Letchworth State Park
Castile, NY 14427-1124
(716) 493-3600

This challenging, but highly rewarding, trail is located about an hour south of Rochester near Letchworth State Park. The adventure begins with the drive south along Interstate 390. As you head into the Genesee Valley, a panorama of patchwork farms and forests spreads before you. Route 436, heading west from Nunda, parallels the original location of the Genesee Valley Canal. From 1852 until 1877, 17 locks lifted this canal over the hill from Nunda to Portageville. As you drive west on Route 436, be on the lookout on the north side for the many stone locks in various states of preservation.

Portage High Bridge still carries trains over Letchworth Gorge.

The trail begins north of Portageville, parallel to the Genesee River. It's a narrow path up a hill that once was part of Portageville Road. As you ride up the hill, the abandoned roadbed will widen but it continues to be a strenuous peddle.

After crossing railroad tracks you'll follow Portageville Road back to Route 436, then take Parade Grounds Road until intersecting the abandoned railroad bed trail. The railroad was abandoned because of difficulty in keeping the route open. It was often blocked by landslides down the steep banks of Letchworth Gorge. Even though the railroad is gone, nature has continued her erosive ways. Landslides have wiped out the original rail bed. You can take a short side trip west along the rail bed to see a waterfall as a creek feeds into the river. The view is spectacular at any time of the year. (See "Side Trip" under Trail Directions.)

The Parade Grounds is a picnic and playground area in Letchworth State Park, off Route 436. During the Civil War, it was an actual infantry parade grounds. From this point eastward, the trail is a wide, abandoned rail bed, though it continues to be rougher than most converted rail beds. Biking is allowed on this trail from June 1 through October 1. Please don't ride this trail in wet conditions to ensure that it remains open for bicycling. You can avoid the roughest portion of the ride by starting at the Parade Grounds and heading to the east. If you choose to do this, consider riding 0.5 mile west from the Parade Grounds to see the waterfall as part of your outing.

NOTE: On the southern end of this trail, within Letchworth State Park, biking is allowed on a trial basis. The policy will be reevaluated in 1999, and biking could be eliminated in this section. Please obey all posted regulations to assure that this trail stays open for all to enjoy.

Bed & Breakfasts: Highbridge Inn B&B, 203 Portageville Road, Portageville, (716) 468-2611

Glen Iris Inn, 7 Letchworth State Park, Castile, (716) 493-2622, also a restaurant serving three meals daily

Broman's Genesee Falls Inn, corner of Main and Hamilton Streets, Portageville, (716) 493-2484

Edgerley B&B, 9303 Creek Road, Hunt, (716) 468-2149

Bike Shop:	Swain Ski and Sports, 131 Main Street, Geneseo. bike rentals, (800) 836-8460
Campground:	Camping and cabins are available at Letchworth State Park, (800) 456-2267

Distance between roads:

Route 436 to Parade Grounds	2.0 miles
Parade Grounds to Route 408	6.1 miles
Route 408 to Creek Road	1.4 miles

Trail Directions

- From the grass parking area on Route 436, head uphill (SW) toward the "Road Closed" sign. The trail is narrow and marked with the yellow blazes of the Finger Lakes Trail. (Ignore the "No Bikes" sign – you will be staying on the abandoned roadbed rather than following the Finger Lakes Trail where bikes are prohibited.)
- At 0.2 mile the yellow blazes of the Finger Lakes Trail bear left. You should bear right, staying on the wide abandoned roadbed as it continues uphill.
- Cross active railroad tracks, watching carefully for trains. The bridge to your left is Portage High Bridge which still carries several freight trains daily. The metal structure replaced the wooden bridge which burned in 1875.
- Continue straight on Portageville Road for a mile until it reaches Route 436. Along the way, pass Highbridge Inn B&B on your left and further down, notice the valley view to your right.
- At Route 436, turn left onto Parade Grounds Road.
- Pass the Parade Grounds parking lot on the left.
- Watch for the intersection of the rail bed trail. Turn right to follow the rail bed.

  [**Side Trip:** A left on the rail bed leads to a spectacular waterfall in 0.5 mile. Across the river, Deh-Ga-Ya-Soh Creek tumbles down the gorge bank to join the river. You can easily see why it's called Inspiration Falls.]
- At 3.8 miles, pass a yellow gate then cross a dirt road (River Road). The Finger Lakes Trail heads off to the left. Be sure to stay on the wide rail bed, do not follow the yellow blazes from this point east.
- At 4.4 miles you come to another dirt road (Williams Road). The rail bed continues straight but is flooded by a beaver dam and is impassable not far beyond. Turn left and follow Williams Road.

- At 4.9 miles cross Short Tract Road and continue straight, again on the rail bed.
- Notice old canal lock #60 on your left at 5.5 miles. This lock was the composite type whose sides were lined with wood. Some of the original wood members are still visible.
- Continue straight on the old rail bed as the Finger Lakes Trail branches off to the right. (On the right along the FLT is old canal lock #59.)
- Head downhill and cross Oakland Road.
- Jog to the right to continue on the rail bed across the road.
- Head uphill on the trail past the "Genesee Valley Greenway" sign.
- At 7.0 miles, cross Picket Line Road.
- At 7.6 miles, cross Hay Road.
- Cross Route 408 after 8.1 miles. Parking is available here.
- At the golf course, stay on the marked trail as you skirt close to the club house. Pass the first tee and a driving range. The rail trail continues on a straight course but you have to make a slight detour to avoid riding directly through the putting green.
- At 8.9 miles, cross Pentagass Road.
- Cross a creek on a wooden bridge. Reach Nunda Junction where the trail to Nunda heads off to the right. Bear left.
- End at the parking area on Creek Road.

Date Bicycled: ______________

Notes:

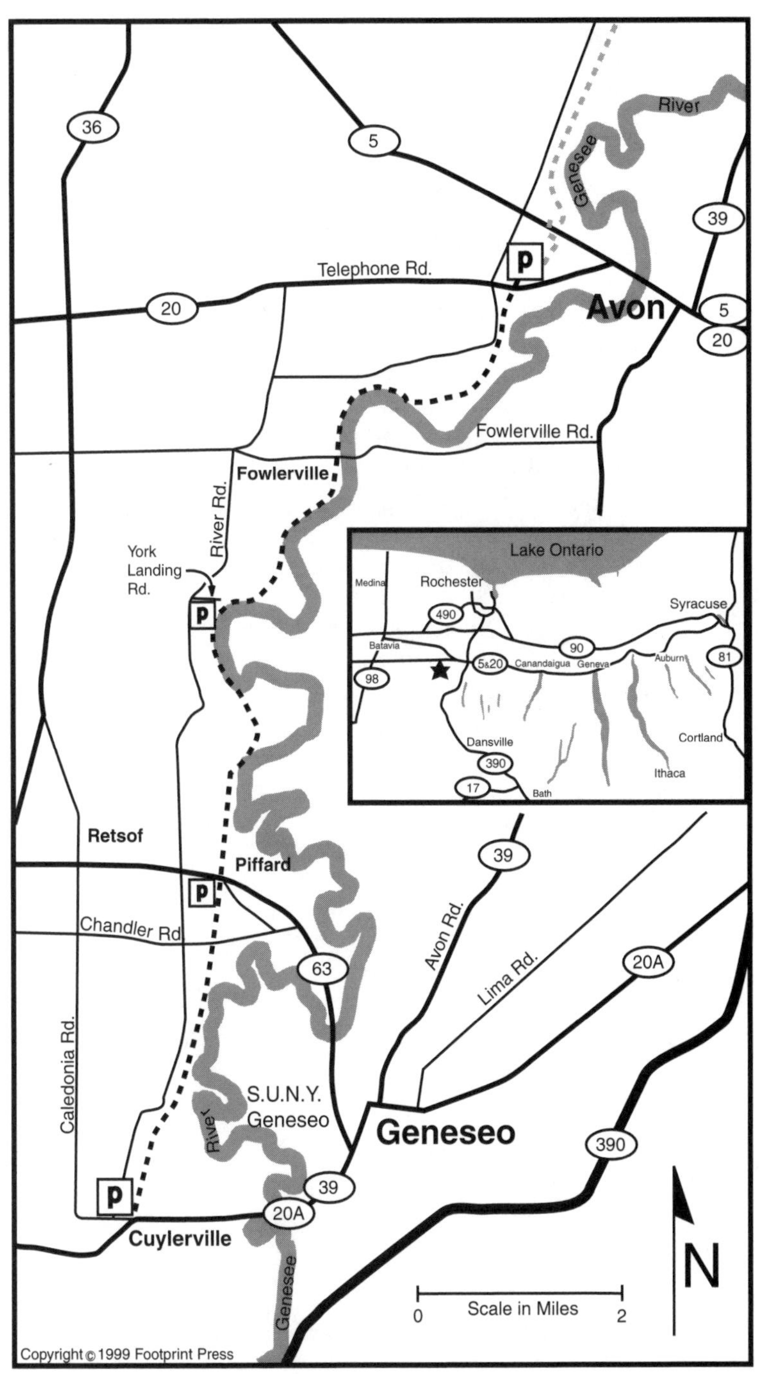

Genesee Valley Greenway - Cuylerville to Avon

10.
Genesee Valley Greenway Cuylerville to Avon

Location: North of Mount Morris, Livingston County

Directions: From Route 390 take Route 20A west through Geneseo. About a mile south of Geneseo, bear right (W) on Routes 39 and 20A. The grass and gravel parking area will be on the northern side of Routes 39 and 20A, just before the sharp left bend in Cuylerville.

Alternative Parking: Yard of Ale Canal House Inn, 3226 Genesee Street (Route 63, 3 miles west of Geneseo, near Flats Road)
At the end of York Landing Road, a side road off River Road
Route 20 (Telephone Road), 0.9 mile west of where Routes 5 and 20 split (west of Avon)

Riding Time: 2 hours

Length: 12.6 miles one way

Difficulty:

Surface: Crushed stone, mowed grass, and packed dirt

Trail Markings: White, metal "Genesee Valley Greenway" signs and yellow metal gates at road crossings

Uses:  

Dogs: OK on leash

Admission: Free

Contact: Friends of the Genesee Valley Greenway, Inc.
P.O. Box 42
Mount Morris, NY 14510
(716) 658-2569
http://www.netacc.net/~fogvg

Regional Wildlife Manager
N.Y.S. Department of Environmental Conservation
6274 East Avon-Lima Road
Avon, New York 14414
(716) 226-2466
http://www.dec.state.ny.us

Forget your preconception of a converted railroad trail. On this segment you're in for some pleasant surprises. Rather than proceeding straight as an arrow, the trail meanders to follow the sweeping curves of the Genesee River, and it's not particularly flat. Not that it's hilly, but it does have lots of little hills and dales, which make the ride interesting. The bed is well packed, so this off-road trail is fairly easy to pedal. There are some natural challenges which the Genesee Valley Greenway is hoping to have resolved soon. Until a bridge is built, you'll have to cross a small creek 1.2 miles in. Just south of the York Landing Road parking area, Mother Nature has created some washout areas. They are temporarily barricaded until the washouts are repaired.

It's hard to match the views along this trail in the spring and summer. But give it a try when the trees are bare to get the full view of the winding Genesee River and the dramatic eroded gorges as water rushes to the river. You'll even pass remains of the cut-stone Lock 5 and several ponds that originally served as turning basins for the Genesee Valley Canal.

The Genesee River begins its northward journey as a small stream in a farmer's field in Pennsylvania and flows 147 miles to Lake Ontario. Native Americans fished the river's waters and traveled its length by canoe. Early settlers used its power to grind grain into flour and to saw trees into lumber. Later, industrial mills harnessed the power to forge iron into parts and weave cotton into cloth. Today the river is a source of recreation and beauty, and its power is still used to generate electricity. The dam at Mount Morris manages the flow of this important waterway.

This country ramble takes you past fields of many varieties, lots of farm lanes, and plenty of wild animals. We had spectacular close-up looks at a coyote and a fox, as well as the more mundane squirrels, deer, geese, cows, horses, and even a cat.

As you bike along, note the presence of stately old oak trees standing right in the middle of a number of farm fields. Years ago, red oak and shagbark hickory were the dominant trees in the forests of upstate New York. But, by the early 1900s, the forest cover was down to ten percent of its original level, as farmers cleared land for fields and harvested the lucrative lumber. A few oaks were spared. Their broad canopy provided shade for farmers and their animals as they toiled in the fields. Some of these old oaks are more than 200 years old.

This public trail is ours to enjoy thanks to the Friends of the Genesee Valley Greenway, the Department of Environmental Conservation, and N.Y.S. Office of Parks, Recreation, and Historic Preservation (O.P.R.H.P.).

Distance between parking areas:	
Route 20A and 39 to Route 63	3.8 miles
Route 63 to River Road	2.9 miles
River Road to Route 20	5.9 miles

Trail Directions

- From the Route 20A and 39 parking lot, head north along the trail bed. (The National Hotel, serving dinners every day but Monday, is 100 yards from the trailhead. Parking is available and it is a good place for drinks and food after a ride.)
- Pass a large swamp pond in 0.6 mile.
- Head right (E) 25 feet before a small stream to cross through the stream feeding the Genesee River at 1.2 miles. A bridge is planned for this crossing.
- At 1.6 miles there is a great view of Geneseo to the east where trees have been cleared for the electric lines.
- Cross Chandler Road at 3.1 miles. The area to your left was once a Tuscarora Indian village called O-Ha-Gi.
- At 3.8 miles, cross Route 63. Parking is available at the Yard Of Ale Restaurant, which serves lunches and dinners daily.
- Further on, Salt Creek flows through a culvert under the rail bed.
- Watch for narrow spots in the rail bed due to erosion. Your way may be blocked by barricades if the washouts have yet to be repaired.
- At 6.7 miles, pass a pond on the left, then a parking area at the end of York Landing Road off River Road. The ponds you pass along the way were once turning basins along the canal.
- Along the trail several culverts divert water under the rail bed as water makes its way to the river.
- Cross Fowlerville Road. You've come 9.3 miles.
- At 10.7 miles, the remains of Lock 5, built around 1840, are on the left.
- The trail jogs to the left at a farm lane.
- This portion of trail ends at the parking lot on the northern side of Route 20.

  [See Trail #13, the Genesee Valley Greenway – Scottsville Trail, to lengthen your ride. From Route 20 the trail continues north through a field via a mowed grass path to Route 5. To cross Route 5 you must climb a steep embankment, carry bicycles over guardrails and repeat

the procedure on the other side of the road. Genesee Valley Greenway plans to install serpentine ramps on each side of Route 5. Once past Route 5, the ride is clear and easy all the way to the Conrail tracks north of Scottsville.]

Date Bicycled: ______________

Notes:

Rattlesnake Hill Wildlife Management Area

The Rattlesnake Hill Wildlife Management Area is a 5,100-acre tract of high elevation land. The land was purchased in the 1930s under the Federal Resettlement Administration when the depletion of the farmland made farming the area unprofitable. The area was turned over to the D.E.C. to be managed as a wildlife habitat.

Don't let the name of this area scare you away. Yes, there are Timber Rattlesnakes in the area, but they are shy creatures who stick to the more remote areas. By staying on trails and roads, your chances of finding one are extremely remote.

As a wildlife management area, Rattlesnake Hill is open to hunting, so be sure to wear bright colors if you venture out during hunting season. The animals found here include white-tailed deer, wild turkey, ruffed grouse, gray squirrel, cottontail rabbit, snowshoe hare, mink, beaver, raccoon, and waterfowl.

This area has both natural and man-made ponds and several streams. Some of the larger ponds are stocked annually with trout. Sugar Creek, Hovey Brook, and Canaseraga Creek are known as trout waters.

Ebert Road is a seasonal road that is closed from November 15 to April 1. If you're heading out in the winter, Ebert Road becomes part of your trail. Camping is not allowed in Rattlesnake Hill Wildlife Management Area except by organized groups during non-hunting seasons by written permit from the Regional Wildlife Manager.

Bed & Breakfast: Kathleen's Country Estate B&B, 7989 Union Corners Road, Dansville, (716) 658-4441

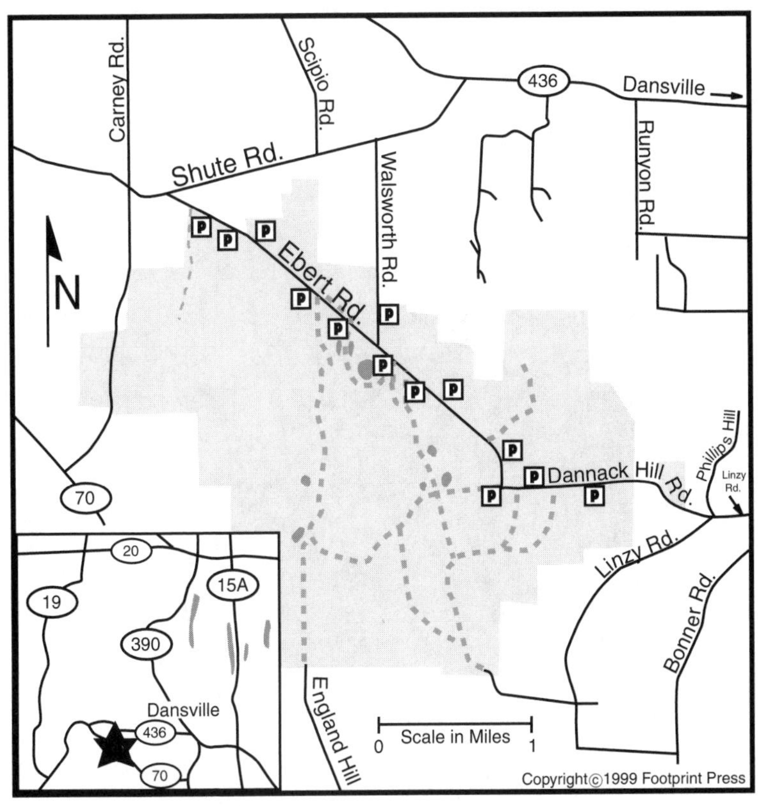

Rattlesnake Hill Wildlife Management Area

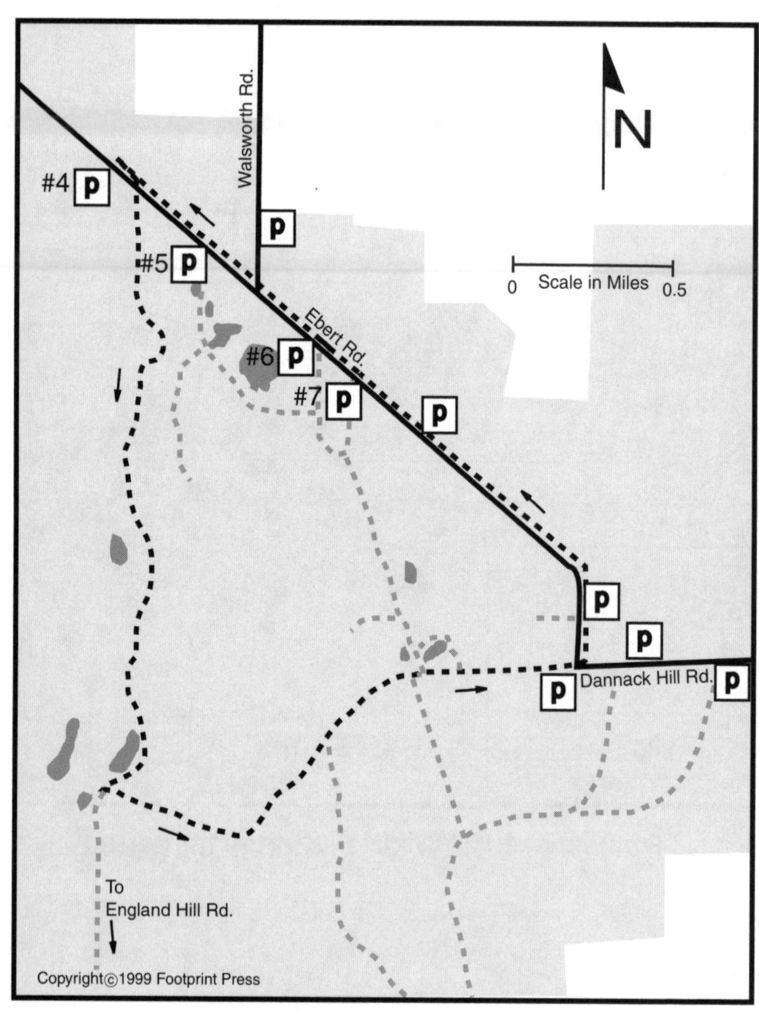

Rattlesnake Hill - Bike Loop

11.
Rattlesnake Hill – Bike Loop

Location: Off Ebert Road (west of Dansville), Livingston and Allegany Counties

Directions: From Route 54 East, turn right on Ebert Road and park at the 4th parking area. (Parking areas are not numbered – simply count as you pass them heading east from Route 54. Be sure to count parking areas on both sides of Ebert Road.)

Alternative Parking: The parking area at the barrier on Dannack Hill Road, near the intersection with Ebert Road.

Hiking Time: 3 hours

Biking Time: 1 hour

Length: 5 mile loop

Difficulty:

Surface: Parallel hard packed dirt tracks (jeep trail) and dirt road

Trail Markings: None

Uses:

Dogs: OK on leash

Admission: Free

Contact: Regional Wildlife Manager
N.Y.S. Department of Environmental Conservation
6274 East Avon-Lima Road
Avon, New York 14414
(716) 226-2466
http://www.dec.state.ny.us

This trail is mostly downhill on great biking trails for the first two thirds of the way. The last leg includes a long, steep uphill on Ebert Road (a dirt road).

Trail Directions

- From the parking area (#4), turn right on Ebert Road.
- In 25 yards, turn right (S) onto the trail. Pass the yellow metal gate.

Riding the trails of Rattlesnake Hill.

- There will be a long, gradual downhill.
- At one mile, pass a small pond on the right, then a few short uphills.
- Turn left at the trail junction. (A wooden storage shed will be on the right. A pond is beyond the shed. The path straight ahead continues to England Hill Road.)
- Now there's a long downhill. At first a stream will be on your left. Then you'll cross over it and the stream will dig a deep gorge on your right.
- Continue straight as a trail heads off to the right.
- Head uphill for 0.3 mile. A hiking trail will cross your path at the top of the hill but continue straight (E).
- The trail will change to a tree canopied gravel road as you head downhill.
- Pass a second hiking trail heading off to the left.
- Pass a yellow metal barrier and you'll be riding on Dannack Hill Road. A parking area is on your right.
- Take a quick left (N) onto Ebert Road. 1.8 miles left to go. Head down hill.
- Stay on the road as you pass a trail off to the left, then a parking area on the right.
- The road bends left and continues downhill.
- Emerge from the tree canopy to an open uphill for 0.7 mile. This can be a hot part of the ride when the sun is out. Some loose gravel portions are difficult biking.
- Pass a wooden storage shed, parking area (#7), and trail on the left. The road now gets easier to ride.
- Pass a trail off to the left.
- Pass Walsworth Road on the right and a parking area (#5) and trail on the left.
- End at the parking area (#4) on the left.

Date Bicycled: ______________

Notes:

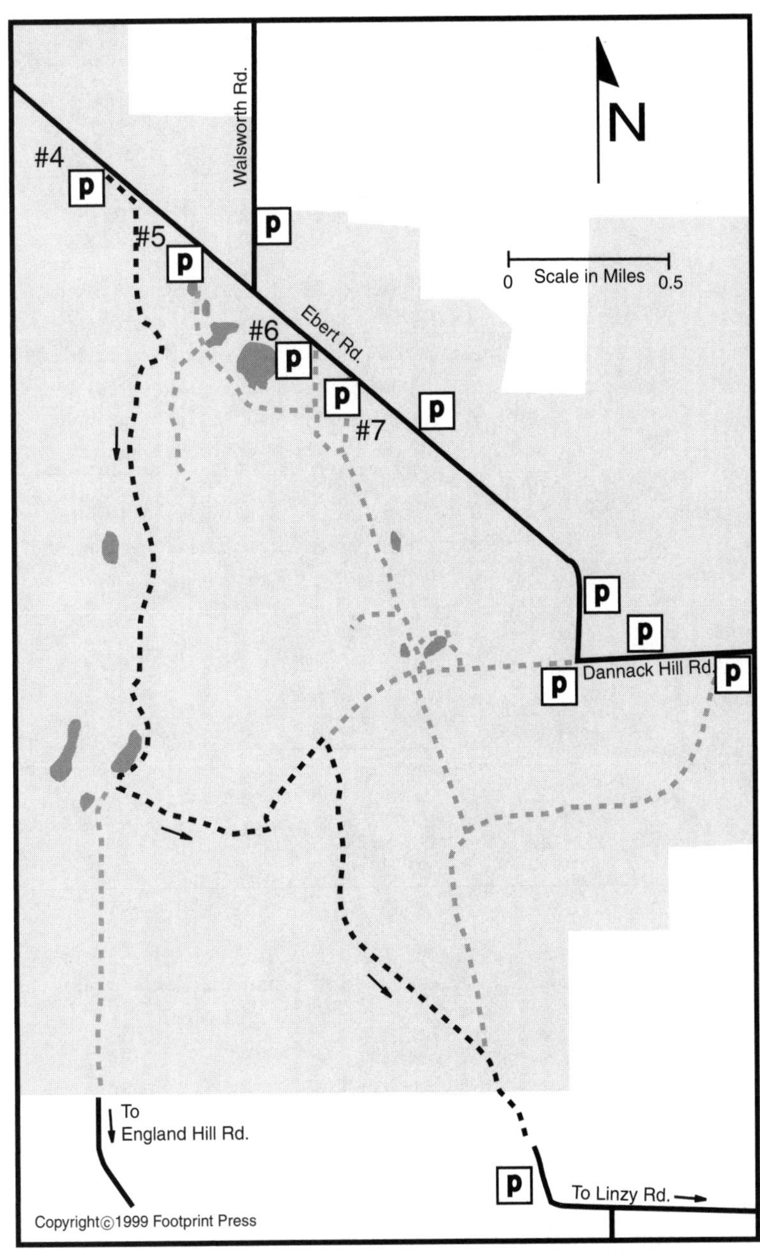

Rattlesnake Hill - Linear Bike Trail

12.
Rattlesnake Hill – Linear Bike Trail

Location: Off Ebert Road, (west of Dansville), Livingston and Allegany Counties

Directions: From Route 54 East, turn right (S) on Ebert Road and park at the 4th parking area. (Parking areas are not numbered – simply count as you pass them heading east from Route 54. Be sure to count parking areas on both sides of Ebert Road.)

Alternative Parking: The south parking area (Follow Linzy Road south; turn right on an unmarked dirt road. Parking is on the left where a barrier blocks the road.)

Hiking Time: 4.5 hours

Biking Time: 1.75 hour

Length: 8.4 miles round trip

Difficulty:

Surface: Parallel hard packed dirt tracks (jeep trail) and dirt road

Trail Markings: None

Uses:

Dogs: OK on leash

Admission: Free

Contact: Regional Wildlife Manager
N.Y.S. Department of Environmental Conservation
6274 East Avon-Lima Road
Avon, New York 14414
(716) 226-2466
http://www.dec.state.ny.us

This trail has gradual hills. The biking path is two hard packed dirt tracks on an abandoned roadbed.

Trail Directions

- From the parking area (#4), turn right on Ebert Road.
- In 25 yards, turn right onto the trail. Pass the yellow metal gate.

- There will be a long, gradual downhill.
- At 1 mile, pass a small pond on the right, then a few short uphills.
- Turn left at the trail junction. (A wooden storage shed will be on the right. A pond is beyond the shed. The path straight ahead continues to England Hill Road.)
- Next there's a long downhill. At first a stream will be on your left. Then you'll cross over it and see the deep gorge dug by the stream on your right.
- Turn right at the next trail intersection. The woods will recede away from the trail leaving a wide, open area full of wildflowers. The hills in this section are gradual.
- Pass a grass path off to the left.
- Head downhill into a serene, shaded gully.
- At the yellow metal barrier, turn around and retrace your path back to the parking lot.

  [The adventurous could continue straight past the barricade on a dirt road. Turn left on Linzy Road, a left (big uphill) on Dannack Hill Road, then a right on Ebert Road to return to the parking area. This loop of 9.6 miles has some challenging hills.]

Date Bicycled: ____________

Notes:

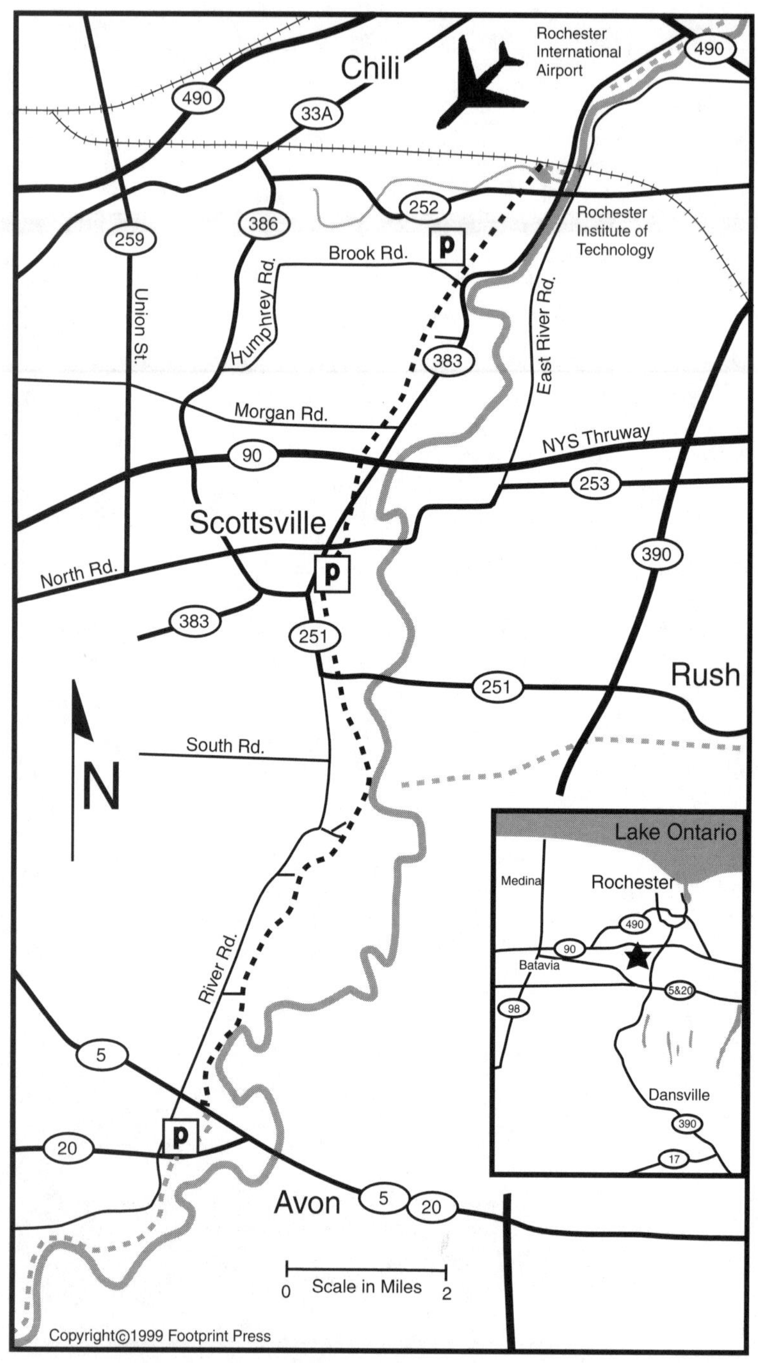

Genesee Valley Greenway - Scottsville

13.
Genesee Valley Greenway Scottsville

Location: Scottsville, Monroe County

Directions: From the Henrietta Exit (exit #44) on the New York State Thruway (Interstate 90), head south on Route 390. At the Route 251 exit, turn right (W) and follow Route 251 to the Canawaugus Park parking lot (on the right just before entering Scottsville).

Alternative Parking: Trail intersection on Brook Road

Riding Time: 2.5 hours

Length: 15.8 round trip, north
15.2 miles round trip, south

Difficulty: 

Surface: Cinder path

Trail Markings: White, metal "Genesee Valley Greenway" signs and yellow metal gates at road crossings

Uses: 

Dogs: OK on leash

Admission: Free

Contact: Friends of the Genesee Valley Greenway, Inc.
P.O. Box 42
Mount Morris, NY 14510
(716) 658-2569
http://www.netacc.net/~fogvg

Regional Wildlife Manager
N.Y.S. Department of Environmental Conservation
6274 East Avon-Lima Road
Avon, New York 14414
(716) 226-2466
http://www.dec.state.ny.us

From Canawaugus Park you can head north for 7.9 miles to the active Conrail tracks north of Route 252. This option takes you past the

Dumpling Hill Lock #2, one of the best-preserved locks on the Genesee Valley Canal that operated from 1840 to 1878. The canal's original 115 locks were made of either wood, a combination of wood and stone, or all stone. Over the years, the wood rotted and most locks deteriorated or were lost altogether. But this 90-foot-long, 15-foot-wide lock is all stone and well preserved. Each lock had a lock keeper and sometimes a lock house. The Dumpling Hill Lock had a house, which was located west of the canal near Coates Road.

There will be a trail at the north end connecting the Genesee Valley Greenway to Scottsville Road (Route 383), but there is no parking area. Plans are underway to develop a parking area in 1999.

You can also head south from Canawaugus Park for 7.6 miles to Route 5. It's a steep climb up to Route 5 from the trail. Serpentine ramps are planned for 1999 to make the climb easier. This ride is more remote, passing through lush farmlands. See Trail # 10 for the continuation of Genesee Valley Greenway south of Route 5. Whichever direction you choose, the trail has an easy-riding, hard-packed cinder base.

From the parking area at Canawaugus Park, look across to the north side of Oatka Creek to see an old feeder gate for the Genesee Valley Canal. A feeder gate consisted of a lock, dam, and tollhouse.

Bed & Breakfast:	Doubling Hills Inn, 2262 Scottsville Road, Scottsville, (716) 234-7878
Ice Cream:	Rocco's Ice Cream Parlor, 30 Main Street, Scottsville, (716) 889-2830
	Scottsville Ice Cream, Scottsville Road (Route 383), Scottsville

Trail Directions – North

- Begin by crossing Oatka Creek on the plate girder (former Pennsylvania Railroad) bridge known locally as the "George Bridge." You are heading northeast on the trail.
- Cross Route 253 and pass Rodney Farms, a thoroughbred horse farm, on the right.
- At Route 383 bear left as a mowed path leads up to the road.
- Cross the road with care, being certain that you can see oncoming traffic far enough ahead for a safe crossing.

- Turn right, following the shoulder of Route 383. (Serpentine ramps are planned for 1999.)
- On the left side is a small graveyard with the gravestone of Joseph Morgan, a Revolutionary War captain. He is credited with being the first settler in Chili in 1792.
- Watch for the trail on the left heading back into the woods. Lift your bike over the guardrail and head downhill.
- Pass under the New York State Thruway.
- Cross a gravel driveway.
- Cross Morgan Road.
- Pass under two sets of power lines.
- Cross several farm lanes.
- Reach Dumpling Hill Lock.
- Overlook horse farms as you ride high on the rail bed.
- Cross Brook Road at 5.9 miles.
- Pass an underground gas pipeline.
- At 7.2 miles, watch for the "W" carved in a metal post on the right. It signaled the train conductor to blow the whistle as they approached a road crossing.
- Cross Ballantyne Road (Route 252). You are near the airport so don't be startled if a jet rumbles overhead.
- Pass a swamp on the right.
- You'll see Black Creek on the right as it heads toward the Genesee River. You're actually riding on a culvert where the waters of Black Creek are diverted under what used to be the Genesee Valley Canal.
- The trail ends at 7.9 miles at the active Conrail tracks. (A 0.4-mile trail to the right to Scottsville Road (Route 383) and a parking area will be developed in 1999.) Turn around and retrace your route.

Trail Directions – South

- From the Canawaugus Park parking lot, head southwest, away from "George Bridge."
- Cross several farm field access paths and a private driveway.
- At 1.0 mile, cross Route 251.
- Cross a bridge at 2.1 miles.
- At 2.6 miles, you'll see the old Lehigh Valley Railroad trestle spanning the Genesee River. Someday in the future, this bridge will link the Genesee Valley Greenway to the Lehigh Valley Trail. Also, pass an abandoned gravel pit area on the right (W).
- Cross a farm road.
- Pass a beaver pond.

- At 4.2 miles, cross a gated entrance to a farmer's fields labeled with a large "Warning – No Trespassing" sign.
- Cross a road.
- Watch carefully to see if you can find the trestle of the abandoned Peanut Branch of the New York Central Railroad. Being a small line earned it the nickname Peanut Branch.
- Cross several farm lanes and underground gas pipelines.
- At 7.4 miles, pass between the stone trestle of the abandoned Erie Railroad that runs east–west. (There is a path on each side.)
- Reach the steep climb to Route 5. Parking is not available here so turn around or continue south using descriptions from Trail #10.

Date Bicycled: ______________

Notes:

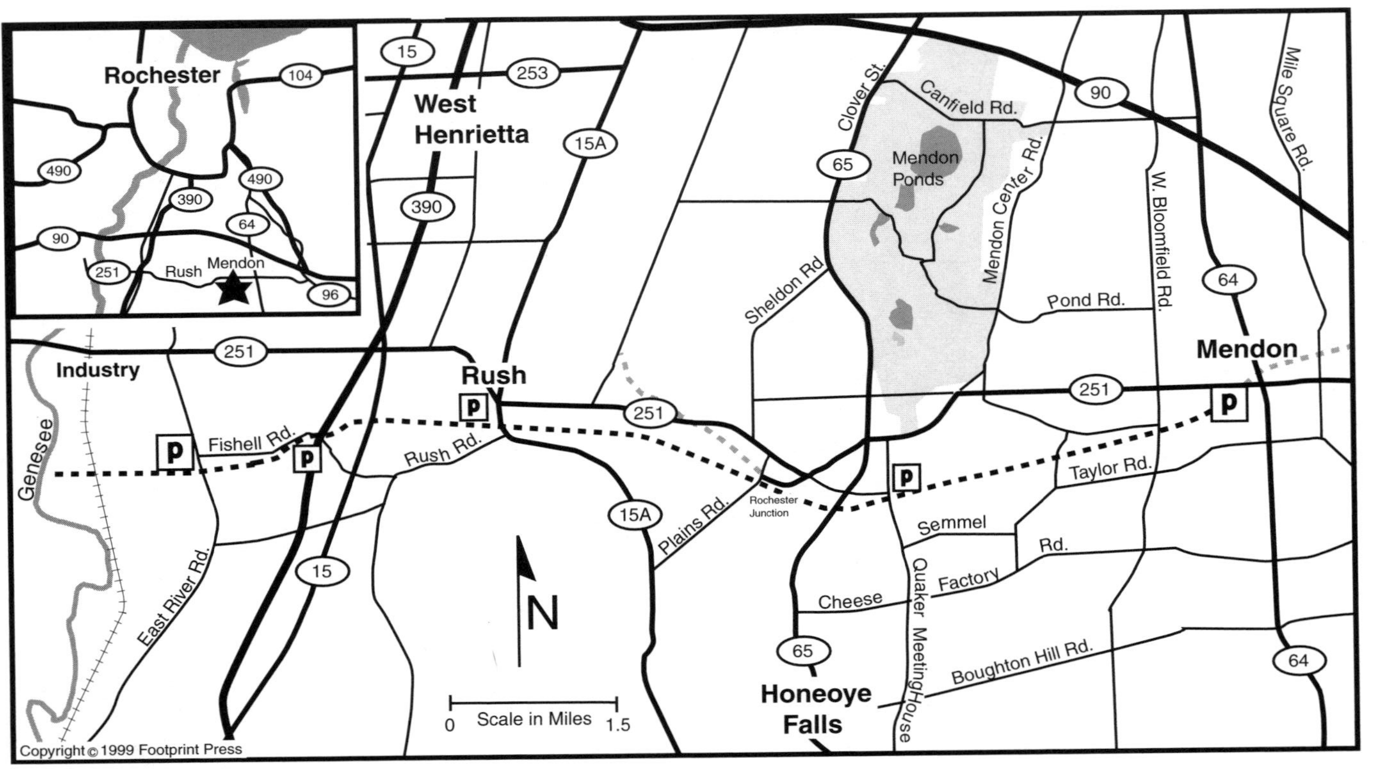

Mendon - Lehigh Valley Trail

14.
Mendon – Lehigh Valley Trail

Location: Mendon, Monroe County

Directions: From Route 390, follow Route 251 east to the village of Mendon. Park at the Honeoye Falls – Mendon Youth Baseball Field on the south side of Route 251 (across from Ye Mendon Tavern)

Alternative Parking: East side of Quaker Meeting House Road
Rush Veterans Memorial Park, Route 15A, Rush
Honeoye Creek Fishing Access, Fishell Road, under Interstate 390
East River Road, south of Fishell Road, Rush (potential endpoint)

Riding Time: 1 hour and 45 minutes

Length: 12.5 miles one way

Difficulty:

Surface: Cinder and stone

Trail Markings: Black, blue, & white metal signs saying "Monroe County Lehigh Valley Trail," with a picture of a black diamond train

Uses:  

Dogs: OK

Admission: Free

Contact: The Mendon Foundation
P.O. Box 231
Mendon, NY 14506

The Mendon – Lehigh Valley Trail is for the rough and ready. The Mendon Foundation is four years into their five-year, trail development plan. A new cinder surface, additional bridges, drainage repairs, and signs are all planned. The current trail has a stony bed, which makes for a bumpy ride, dirt mounds at the road crossings that any BMX rider will enjoy, and puddles in which to splash. But, don't pass up this ride if you want country solitude through woods and fields, because this path has that also.

The Lehigh Valley Railroad got its start in the coal mines of Pennsylvania. Valleys cut by the Lehigh River became channels for transporting the inexpensive, high-grade, anthracite or hard coal from the mines to Rochester and Buffalo. The Rochester station still stands on Court Street across from the Rundel Library. Rochester Junction in Mendon was a major intersection where trains ran west to Buffalo, south to Hemlock Lake, and north to Rochester. Remains of the old rail station platform are visible today.

Approaching the redecked trestle on Lehigh Valley Trail.

The Lehigh Valley Railroad was built in 1891 to capture some of the lucrative "black diamond" (as coal was nicknamed) freight business. The train, dubbed the "Black Diamond Express," was advertised as the "Handsomest Train in the World." In 1896, it began passenger service between Buffalo and New York. This plush train offered smoking rooms, a polished-mahogany library, velvet upholstery, and beveled French-plate mirrors. The engine was an iron horse manufactured by Baldwin. This train could reach speeds of 80 miles per hour and maintained its schedule 92% of the time. Honeymooners often rode in luxury to Niagara Falls.

In the 1920s, anthracite coal began to lose favor as a home-heating fuel. Homeowners discovered the ease and low cost of gas and oil. By the 1930s, the Depression and competition from cars and trucks steadily pulled business away from the trains. Ownership of the rail line changed several times until 1974, when the business was dismantled for scrap iron and parts. Today, the county of Monroe owns the railroad bed. The trail is being developed by the towns of Mendon and Rush, the Monroe County Parks Department, and especially a non-profit land trust organization called Mendon Foundation and many volunteers. As you ride this trail, think back to the times when steam locomotives hauled coal and the "Black Diamond" transported passengers in luxury. Keep your eyes to the ground, and you may be lucky enough to find a piece of "black diamond" from a bygone era.

The Mendon Foundation is using an innovative program to beautify the road intersections of the Lehigh Valley Trail. Their "Adopt an Intersection" program gives landscapers advertising opportunities in exchange for planting and caring for vegetation where the trail crosses roads. Likewise, they've solicited donations from residents for beautification of the Route 251 parking lot. This win/win situation certainly benefits the whole community.

This trail extends east from Route 251, ending in Victor. Connect the route described here with the Victor – Lehigh Valley Trail (#15) for a 15.3-mile adventure (one way).

Distances between parking areas:	
Route 251 to Quaker Meeting House Road	3.4 miles
Quaker Meeting House Road to Route 15A	4.5 miles
Route 15A to Fishell Road	1.9 miles
Fishell Road to East River Road	1.3 miles

Trail Directions

- From the Route 251 parking lot, head southwest past wooden posts on a cinder and stone path.
- Cross a small cement bridge over a creek.
- Cross West Bloomfield Road.
- Walk or ride over a dirt mound and through a short stretch of ballast stone.
- Parallel Irondequoit Creek on your left for a short while.
- Cross Chamberlain Road.
- Traverse several short sections of ballast stone.
- Ride around and through a series of wet areas and cross another dirt mound.
- Cross Quaker Meeting House Road.
- Wind down a mowed path, cross a small stream, and climb to cross Route 65. (Parking is not available at Route 65.)
- Note the old railroad bridge to your left as an abandoned Conrail line merges with the Lehigh.
- On the right pass an old cement platform and switching mechanism. This area was once Rochester Junction where the Lehigh and Conrail trains crossed.
- Cross Plains Road. This section of trail was newly topped with crushed cinder in 1998.
  [**Side Trip:** Just past the white house at 275 Plains Road, another railroad bed heads northwest for 0.9 mile to a parking area along Route 251. The trail north of Route 251 is cleared for 1.8 miles, but deep pumice stones make it impassable for bicycles.]
- Cross over a large metal trestle bridge spanning Honeoye Creek. This bridge has new decking and railings spanning 160 feet, compliments

of Boy Scout Troop 45 of Rochester, The Monroe County Parks Department, and Mendon Foundation volunteers.

- Emerge onto Park Lane. Honeoye Creek is on your right. There is a picnic area at Rush Veterans Memorial Park.
  [**Note:** A quarter mile to the right (N) are a grocery store and a convenience store at the corner of Route 251.]
- Cross Route 15A next to Rush Creekside Inn. You've come 8 miles so far.
- Cross a second trestle bridge over Honeoye Creek. This 120-foot span was redecked by volunteers from the village of Rush.
- Ride under the Route 15 bridge.
- The trail bends left, parallel to Interstate 390.
- Head downhill to Fishell Road.
- Turn right and ride under Interstate 390, past Honeoye Creek Fishing Access.
- Shortly after the Interstate 390 bridge, bear left and head uphill on a gravel path.
- Cross a driveway.
- Cross East River Road. This is the last parking area along the trail. Beyond this point the bridges have not been resurfaced. If you continue the remaining 1.3 miles to the Genesee River, use caution. Also, this area is not recommended for children. Future plans include extending this trail over the Genesee River to connect with the Genesee Valley Greenway.
- Cross a bridge over the Conrail tracks. The bridge is passable but not redecked, use caution.
- Cross a bridge over a swamp. The bridge is passable but not redecked, use caution.
- Pass a large stone abutment. A large trestle used to span over the Genesee River from this point.
- Head downhill and then the path becomes a narrow mowed strip through woods.
- The trail ends at the old bridge over the Genesee River. This bridge is not passable.

Date Bicycled: ______________

Notes:

Rides in Ontario County

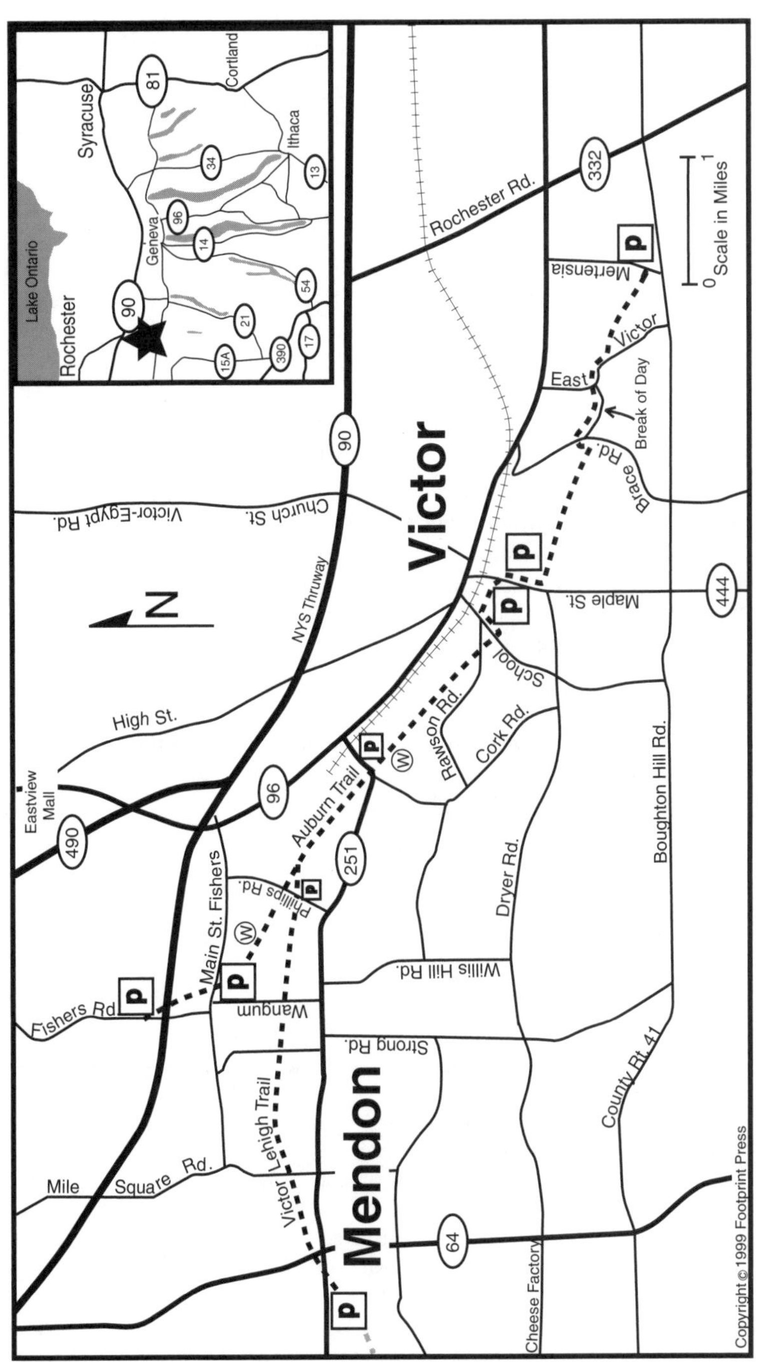

Victor - Lehigh Valley Trail and Auburn Trail

15.
Victor – Lehigh Valley Trail

Location:	Victor and Mendon, Ontario and Monroe Counties
Directions:	From Route 96, just south of New York State Thruway exit 45, head west on Main Street Fishers. Turn south on Phillips Road. Park along Phillips Road at the trail crossing closest to Victor-Mendon Road. The trail crossing just to the north is the Auburn Trail (see Trail #16).
Alternative Parking:	At the Honeoye Falls - Mendon Youth Baseball Field on Route 251, just west of the four corners in Mendon (across from Ye Mendon Tavern).
Riding Time:	30 minutes
Length:	2.8 miles one way
Difficulty:	
Surface:	Cinder, dirt, gravel, and mowed grass path
Trail Markings:	11-inch green-and-yellow "Victor Hiking Trail" signs at road crossings
Uses:	 
Dogs:	OK
Admission:	Free
Contact:	Victor Hiking Trails, Inc. 85 East Main Street Victor, NY 14564 (716) 234-8226 http://www.ggw.org/freenet/v/vht/

Here's another new trail to explore, thanks to a cooperative effort. The Victor – Lehigh Valley Trail used to be deep in ballast stone, but in the winter of 1997, the Victor Department of Transportation graded the path to plow away most of the ballast. Eastman Kodak Company donated fly ash for the treadway. Monroe County installed the fly ash and supplied signs. Coordination and maintenance are being provided by Victor Hiking Trails in Victor.

The easternmost end of the trail connects with the Auburn Trail (#16) where the Lehigh Valley Railroad trestle passes high over the Auburn line. At its western end, the trail continues past the village of Mendon for 12.5 miles, to the Genesee River as the Mendon – Lehigh Valley Trail (#14).

The Lehigh Valley Railroad got its start in the coal mines of Pennsylvania. Valleys cut by the Lehigh River became channels for transporting the inexpensive, high-grade, anthracite or hard coal from the mines to Rochester and Buffalo. The Rochester station still stands on Court Street across from the Rundel Library.

The Lehigh Valley Railroad was built in 1891 to capture some of the lucrative "black diamond" (as coal was nicknamed) freight business. The train, dubbed the "Black Diamond Express," was advertised as the "Handsomest Train in the World." In 1896 it began passenger service between Buffalo and New York. This plush train offered smoking rooms, a polished mahogany library, velvet upholstery, and beveled French-plate mirrors. The engine was an iron horse manufactured by Baldwin. The train could reach speeds of 80 miles per hour and maintained its schedule 92% of the time. Honeymooners often rode in luxury to Niagara Falls.

In the 1920s, anthracite coal began to lose favor as a home-heating fuel. Homeowners discovered the ease and low cost of gas and oil. By the 1930s, the Depression and competition from cars and trucks steadily pulled business away from the trains. Ownership of the rail line changed several times until 1974 when the business was dismantled for scrap iron and parts.

Bed & Breakfasts: Golden Rule B&B, 6934 Rice Road, Victor, (716) 924-0610

Safari House B&B, 950 Deer Crossing, Victor, (716) 924-0250

Distances between major roads:

Phillips Road to Wangum Road	0.7 mile
Wangum Road to Old Dutch Road	0.4 mile
Old Dutch Road to Mile Square Road	1.0 mile
Mile Square Road to Route 64	0.6 mile
Route 64 to Route 251	0.1 mile

Trail Directions

- From Phillips Road head west along the newly resurfaced rail bed.
- Cross Wangum Road, former site of Fisherville.
- Cross Old Dutch Road. In 0.5 mile there will be a short stretch of ballast stone. Then the path will turn to cinder.
- Cross Mile Square Road.
- Ride across a redecked bridge over Irondequoit Creek. The path will become mowed grass.
- Cross Route 64. The path returns to cinder and gravel.
- Cross a small creek.
- Cross Route 251. (Parking is available here.) The trail does continue on to the Genesee River. See the Mendon – Lehigh Valley Trail (#14).

Date Bicycled: ____________

Notes:

16.
Auburn Trail

Location: Victor, Ontario County

Directions: From Route 96, just south of New York State Thruway exit 45, head west on Main Street Fishers. Turn north on Fishers Road. Ride under the Thruway and park at the trailhead on the east side of Fishers Road at the green-and-yellow sign for "Victor Hiking Trails." There is room for only one car.

Alternative Parking: In back of the Fishers Firehouse on Main Street, Fishers
Victor Volunteer Fireman's Memorial Field, Maple Street, Victor
West side of Mertensia Road at brown sign saying "Farmington – Welcome to Auburn Trail"

Riding Time: 65 minutes

Length: 7.5 miles one way

Difficulty:

Surface: Cinder and mowed-grass path

Trail Markings: 3.5-inch white, diamond shaped, metal markers for "Victor Hiking Trail"
11-inch square, green-and-yellow "Victor Hiking Trail" signs at road crossings
Brown signs for "Farmington – Welcome to Auburn Trail"

Uses:   

Dogs: OK

Admission: Free

Contact: Victor Hiking Trails, Inc.
85 East Main Street
Victor, NY 14564-1397
(716) 234-8226
http://www.ggw.org/freenet/v/vht/

The cobblestone pump house in the village of Fishers.

The Auburn Trail was one of the first trails opened by Victor Hiking Trails. This volunteer group was conceived by the Victor Conservation Board in the 1980s. The first organizational meeting occurred in September 1991, and the Auburn Trail opened in September 1993. The extreme eastern section of the Auburn Trail was developed and is maintained by the town of Farmington.

The Auburn Trail was once the bustling Rochester and Auburn Railroad. No rails or ties remain on the railroad bed; they have been gone for years. At one time, the Auburn was part of the New York Central Railroad System, owned by Cornelius Vanderbilt. It was the main east–west line.

Where the Auburn rail bed is not accessible in the village of Victor, this bikeway detours for a short distance on the old Rochester and Eastern Trolley bed. On your journey, you'll pass a train station from each of these lines. The trolley station will be directly in front of you as you cross Maple Street. The Auburn railroad station is in the Whistle Stop Arcade on Railroad Street.

You will also pass through a spectacular tunnel under the New York State Thruway. The tunnel was built large enough for trains. At another point two former railroads cross, so you will ride under an old railroad trestle that was used by the Lehigh Valley Railroad. See Victor – Lehigh Valley Trail (#15) for information on this trail.

Nature is plentiful along the way. Part of the rail bed is raised to overlook scenic swamp and pond areas. Look carefully as you pedal by, and you may be able to pick some blackberries for a quick snack. The trail abounds with birds, beaver, deer, and muskrats. Geese may even honk as you pass their pens.

History will also surround you. Be sure to watch for the old potato storage building and old rail sidings as you pass through Fishers. Stop to admire the 1845, cobblestone railroad pump house (adjacent to the Fishers firehouse). It's the oldest cobblestone railroad building in the country. Concrete "tombstones" along the way were mileposts for the trains. One marked "S85" denoted that Syracuse was 85 miles away. A "W" in the concrete marker told the engineer that a road crossing was coming and to blow the train's whistle. See if you can find a rectangular concrete box partly buried in the ballast. This battery box was used to power the signals at road crossings if the main power was down.

Please stay on the white-marked railway bed. Other trails intersect this path, but bikes are not permitted on them. There are some remaining "No Trespassing" signs along the way. As long as you stay on the old rail bed, you can ignore them. The rail bed is open for public use from Fishers Road to School Street, from Maple Street to Brace Road, and from East Victor Road to Mertensia Road. Between these railway bed sections you must travel on lightly used roads.

Bed & Breakfasts:	Golden Rule B&B, 6934 Rice Road, Victor, (716) 924-0610
	Safari House B&B, 950 Deer Crossing, Victor, (716) 924-0250
Campground:	Canandaigua KOA Kampground, 5374 Farmington Townline Road, Farmington, (716) 398-3582

Distances between main roads:

Fishers Road to Main Street, Fishers	0.6 mile
Main Street, Fishers to Phillips Road	0.9 mile
Phillips Road to Route 251	1.1 miles
Route 251 to Rawson Road	1.1 miles
Rawson Road to School Street	0.2 mile
School Street to Maple Street (via trolley)	0.6 mile
Maple Street to Whistle Stop	0.4 mile
Whistle Stop to Brace Road	1.2 miles
Brace Road to rail bed on E. Victor Road	0.8 mile
E. Victor Road to Mertensia Road	0.6 mile

Trail Directions (see map on page 95)

- From the trailhead at Fishers Road, head southeast past a brown metal gate, on a mowed path.
- Geese may honk at you from their pen on the left.
- Pass through the tunnel under the New York State Thruway.
- Emerge from the woods along the side yard of a house.
- Cross Main Street, Fishers, and continue across the grass between the Fishers firehouse on your right and the cobblestone pump house on your left.
- A green-and-yellow "Victor Hiking Trails" sign directs you straight ahead, back into the woods.
- Notice the old potato storage building on your right. Look for the water

The Auburn Trail utilizes a tunnel under the New York State Thruway.

ditch from the creek that was used by the cobblestone pump house to provide water for the steam engines.

- Ride around the metal gates on each side of Phillips Road.
- Ride under the old trestle for the Lehigh Valley Railroad. A connecting path is planned to join the Auburn Trail with the Victor – Lehigh Trail (#15).
- Watch for the concrete battery box on the right.
- The cinder path widens. Snapping turtles like to bury their eggs in the cinder banks.
- Pass the metal gates and cross Route 251 (Victor-Mendon Road).
- A red marker for Seneca Trail is on the left. Bikes are not permitted on Seneca Trail. (Hiking on the Seneca Trail is described in *Take A Hike! Family Walks in the Finger Lakes & Genesee Valley Region.*)
- The Seneca Trail (red markers) intersects again.
- Pass the metal gates and cross Rawson Road.
- Turn left onto School Street. (The trail ahead turns into Seneca Trail and heads south toward Ganondagan State Historic Site. It is open to walkers only.)
- Just after the post office, the path turns to asphalt on the right (E) side of School Street.
- Turn right to stay on the asphalt path. This was the trolley line.
- Cross active railroad tracks, then a wooden bridge.
- Arrive on Maple Street at the Victor Volunteer Fireman's Memorial Field sign. (Parking is available here.) Directly across Maple Street is the

old trolley station, which is now a business. Downtown Victor and shops are to the left.

- Turn right (S) on Maple Street. Sidewalks are available on both sides of this busy road.
- Pass stately old homes along Maple Street. Pass East Street.
- Turn left onto the railroad bed just after the sign for the Whistle Stop Arcade. The former Rochester and Auburn train station is on your left.
- Cross through Mickey Finn's Restaurant parking lot toward a metal gate with a "No Motor Vehicles" sign. You'll also find a "Victor Hiking Trails" sign.
- Cross a new housing development road. Ride through a wooded area.
- Victor Hills Golf Course is on the right.
- Turn left onto Brace Road. (The trail ahead, between Brace and East Victor Roads, is a narrow path through close trees. Bikes are not allowed.)
- At the stop sign, turn right onto Break Of Day Road. Note the historic stone house on the left.
- Turn right onto East Victor Road and head uphill.
- Watch for a yellow-and-green "Hiking Trail" sign on the left, just before the power lines that cross East Victor Road, and turn left onto the trail bed.
- Negotiate some tight turns and then a roller-coaster ride on a raised cinder bed.
- Pass a brown sign saying "Farmington – Welcome to Auburn Trail."
- Cross a bridge with chain-link sides over Mud Creek.
- Notice the gorgeous view of the rock-strewn creek to your right. In the spring, look for bluebells.
- A cement pillar "S82" is hidden in the brush on the right (W) side of the trail. This told the train engineer that it was 82 miles to Syracuse.
- The public trail ends at Mertensia Road with parking available.

Date Bicycled: ____________

Notes:

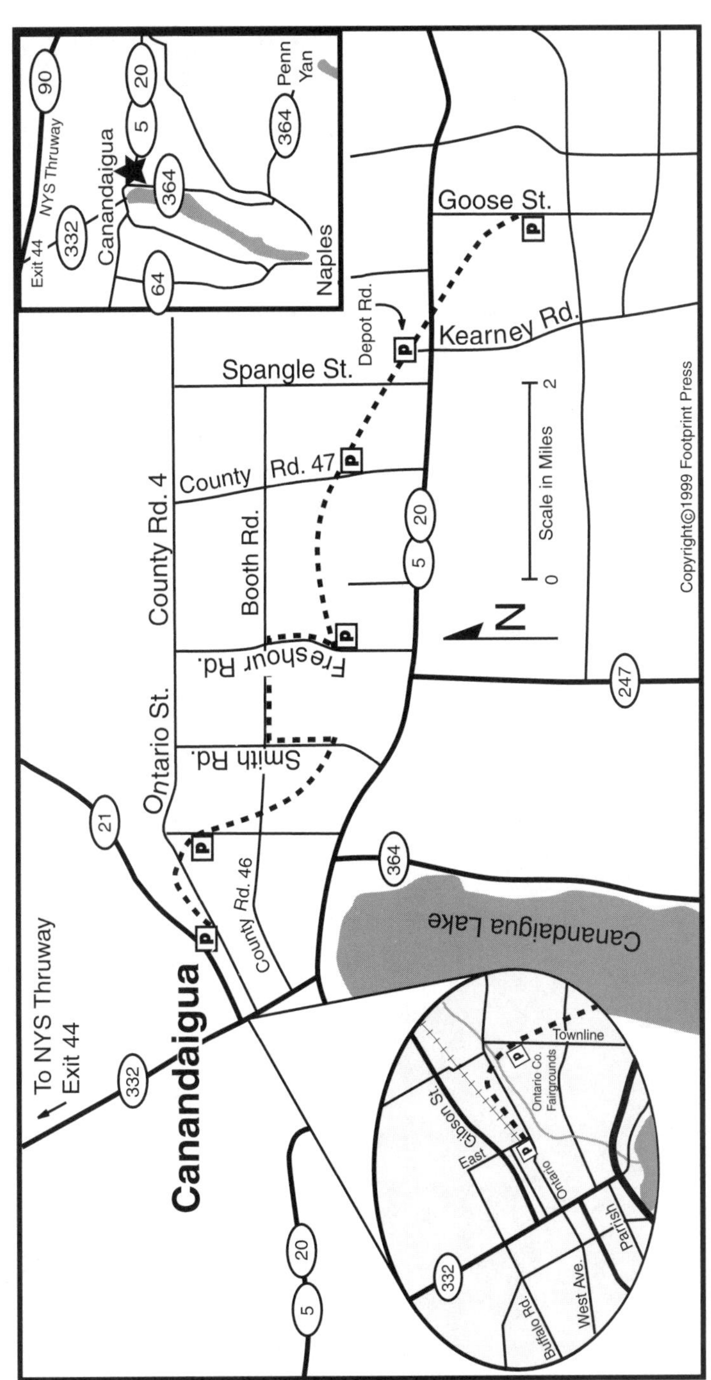

Ontario Pathways Trail

17.

Ontario Pathways Trail

Location: Canandaigua, Ontario County

Directions: From Route 332 in downtown Canandaigua, turn left (E) onto Ontario Street just after the Ontario County Courthouse (a yellow building with a statue on its gold-domed roof). Pass the Ontario County Sheriff and Jail building. Cross active railroad tracks. The parking lot is on the left in front of an old red warehouse.

Alternative Parking: On Townline Road near Ontario County Fairgrounds
Freshour Road
County Road 47
Depot Road

Riding Time: 2 hours

Length: 11 miles one way (or two segments, one 3.4 miles and the other 5.2 miles)

Difficulty:

Surface: Cinder and mowed grass

Trail Markings: Plastic, green-and-white signs that read "Welcome to Ontario Pathways"
Green-and-yellow plastic signs that read "Warning No Motorized Vehicles, No Hunting on Trail, Ontario Pathways, Inc."

Uses: 

Dogs: OK on leash

Admission: Free

Contact: Ontario Pathways
P.O. Box 996
Canandaigua, NY 14424
(716) 394-7968

Ontario Pathways is a grass-roots organization, formed in 1993, of people dedicated to the establishment of public-access trails throughout

Pedaling under a colorful fall canopy on the Ontario Pathways Trail.

Ontario County. They purchased and are working to develop two rail beds abandoned by the Penn Central Corporation. Trains last thundered over this land in 1972, when Hurricane Agnes hit and damaged many of the rails. When complete, these two rail beds will cover 22 miles from Canandaigua southwest to Stanley, and from Stanley north to Phelps. Two other portions, of approximately 4 miles long, of the Ontario Pathways trail are open for public use in addition to the 11 miles described here.

The rail bed you'll be riding started operation in 1851, as the Canandaigua Corning Line and was financed by prominent Canandaigua residents Mark Sibley, John Granger, Oliver Phelps III, and Jared Wilson. But this short line, like many of its cousins, suffered grave financial losses and changed names four times in 14 years. Even the federal government became involved when, in 1862, President Abe Lincoln authorized the expenditure of $50,000 to revive the line so that men and supplies could be moved southward to the Civil War battlefront in Pennsylvania. Recruits rode this line to training centers in Elmira, New York, and Harrisburg, Pennsylvania.

By 1880, Canandaigua became a tourist attraction. Cargo switched from agricultural goods to passengers, as five trains ran daily between Canandaigua and Elmira. But, as with all of the railroads, business faded in the 1950s and 1960s because of competition from cars and trucks. The rail line changed hands many more times, until the merger of Northern Central with New York Central to form the Penn Central in 1968. Penn Central filed for bankruptcy in 1970, and train traffic dwindled even further. When Hurricane Agnes blew through the area in 1972, she damaged bridges, tracks, and rail beds. Penn Central abandoned the line, sold the rails for scrap, and sold the land corridor in 1994 to Ontario Pathways.

For a short distance the Ontario Pathways Trail parallels an active railway.

The trail is a 10-foot-wide swath through lush countryside. We rode it in the fall, pedaling over a bed of colored leaves with the canopy above blazing reds and yellows. It would be a delight to ride this trail in any season except, of course, the snow season when cross-country skis or snowshoes would be more appropriate. This 11-mile stretch of trail consists of two railway bed sections connected by a short road ride. The first section, from Ontario Street to Smith Road, is 3.4 miles of easy riding on hard packed cinder. The road section is 2.5 miles on backcountry roads. Then back to the railway bed section for 5.2 miles. This is a new section of trail and some parts are a little bumpy and rough. They will benefit from the passage of time as snow, rain, and human usage, pack them down. Even so, the trail is rideable and takes you through tranquil farmlands.

Bed & Breakfasts:	Clawson's B&B, 3615 Lincoln Hill Road, Canandaigua, (800) 724-6379
	Morgan Samuels Inn, 2920 Smith Road, Canandaigua, (716) 394-9232
	Oliver Phelps Country Inn, 252 North Main Street, Canandaigua, (800) 724-7397
	Sutherland House B&B, 3179 State Route 21 South, Canandaigua, (800) 396-0375
Bike Shop:	Park Avenue Bike Shop, Parkway Plaza, Route 5 and 20, (716) 398-2300
Campgrounds:	Bristol Woodlands Campground, South Hill Road, Canandaigua, (716) 229-2290
	Canandaigua KOA Kampground, 5374 Farmington Townline Road, Farmington, (716) 398-3582
	Creekside Campsite, Wheeler Station Road, Canandaigua, (716) 657-7746

Distance between major roads:

Ontario Street to East Street	0.3 mile
East Street to Ontario Street	0.9 mile
Ontario Street to Townline Road	0.4 mile
Townline Road to County Road 46	0.8 mile
County Road 46 to Smith Road	1.0 mile
Smith Road to Freshour Road (on roads)	2.5 miles
Freshour Road to County Road 47	1.6 mile
County Road 47 to Depot Road	1.7 mile
Depot Road to Goose Street	1.8 mile

Trail Directions

- From the parking area on Ontario Street head northeast on the trail, away from the city of Canandaigua, parallel to an active set of railroad tracks. If you're lucky, a train will come by.
- Cross East Street.
- Pass a red metal gate. On the left, watch for the cement pillar with "S73" denoting 73 miles to Syracuse.
- After a while, the trail and railroad tracks diverge.
- Head downhill past a red gate. Cross Ontario Street.
- Head uphill then cross a long wooden bridge over Canandaigua Outlet.
- The Ontario County Fair Grounds appears on your right.
- Cross Townline Road near the entrance to the Fair Grounds.
- Cross County Road 46. You've now come 2.4 miles.
- Cross a dirt driveway.
- The first trail section ends at Smith Road. Turn around and retrace your path or continue forward by turning left (N) on Smith Road.
- Turn right (W) onto County Road 46.
- At 5.2 total riding miles (1.7 miles so far on roads), turn right onto Freshour Road.
- In another 0.8 mile, turn left (E) onto the Ontario Pathway Trail. Pass a red metal gate.
- Cross several farm lanes.
- At 7.2 total riding miles, pass a red metal gate, then a farm lane.
- Pass a farm lane, buildings, and a sheep pasture on the left. Continue straight on the trail, passing a farm pond and a farm lane to the right.
- At 7.6 miles, cross County Road 47. Pass a metal gate.
- Cross several farm lanes.
- Pass a red metal gate, cross Spangle Road, then pass another gate.
- At 9.1 miles, bear right heading downhill. Cross a farm lane that goes past old railroad abutments, then head uphill back to the railroad bed.
- You'll see houses on the right and the end of Depot Road where parking is available.
- Cross a farm lane then pass a metal gate.
- At 9.6 miles, cross over Route 5 & 20 on a railroad bridge.
- The trail will dip at a farm lane then crosses a small bridge.
- Cross more farm lanes.
- Pass a metal gate just before reaching the end at Goose Street.

Date Bicycled: _______________

Notes:

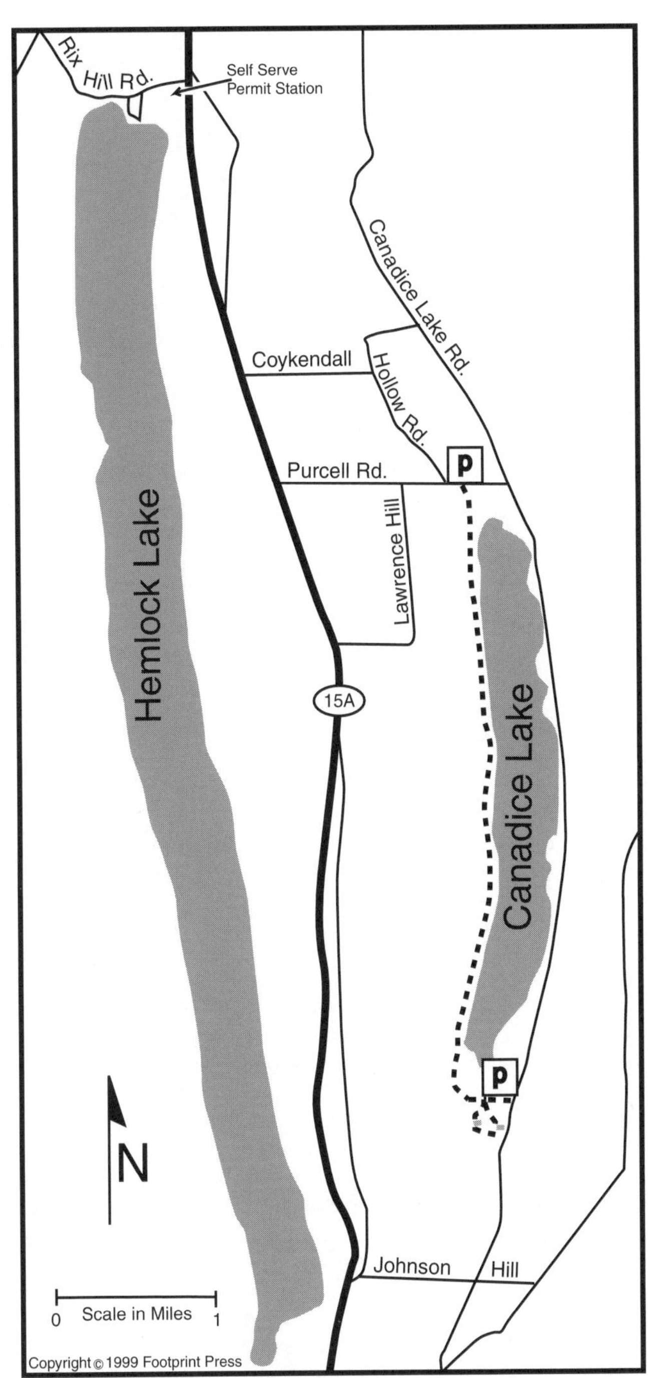

Canadice Lake Trail

18.
Canadice Lake Trail

Location: West side of Canadice Lake, Ontario County
Directions: From Route 15A, head east on Purcell Hill Road at the north end of Canadice Lake. The parking area is east of Hollow Road.
Alternative Parking: Canadice Lake Road, approximately 3.5 miles south of Purcell Hill Road on west side of road (lake side)
Riding Time: 35 minutes
Length: 3.7 miles one way
Difficulty:
Surface: Two lane, gravel, grass
Trail Markings: 12 x 18-inch, green-and-white signs labeled with hiker silhouettes and "Hemlock Canadice Watershed"
Uses:
Dogs: OK on leash
Admission: Free
Contact: City of Rochester, Water and Lighting Bureau
7412 Rix Hill Road
Hemlock, NY 14466
(716) 346-2617

Long ago, Canadice Lake had cottages all along its shore. In 1872, the city of Rochester decided to use Canadice and Hemlock Lakes as a water supply. The first conduit for water was completed in 1876. By 1947, Rochester purchased all of the shoreline property and removed the cottages so that it could preserve the water supply for its growing population. Although it was difficult for the cottage residents to leave their land, this area is now free of the commercialization that is so rampant on the other Finger Lakes. Ninety-foot-deep Canadice Lake is the smallest of the Finger Lakes, but it has the highest elevation, at 1,096 feet, which is one of the reasons it is such a good water supply for the city. Flow from Canadice Outlet Creek is diverted into the northern end of Hemlock Lake. From

Canadice Lake Trail invites you to explore.

there the City of Rochester Water Bureau conditions the water for drinking and sends it north via large pipes.

Early settlers tried to farm around Canadice Lake but found the glacially scoured land ill-suited for farming. Many areas around the lake were too steep or too wet for growing crops.

Today, the Hemlock and Canadice Lakes watershed continues to be Rochester's primary source of drinking water. The watershed covers more than 40,000 acres of land, of which Rochester owns 7,000 acres. A second-growth forest now prospers on the once forested land, and many abandoned farm fields have been reforested with conifers. Bald eagles are now present in the area.

To protect city property and the supply of drinking water, the city asks that all visitors obtain a Watershed Visitor Permit, one of the easiest permits to obtain. Just stop at the visitor's self-serve, permit station located at the north end of Hemlock Lake on Rix Hill Road off Route 15A. There are no fees or forms to fill out, but the permit document details the dos and don'ts to help keep the area pristine, so it's important to read it. Swimming and camping are not permitted. Boats up to 16 feet long with motors up to 10 horsepower are okay. The permit also has a detailed map showing additional hiking trails.

You may also want to continue west on Rix Hill Road to Hemlock Lake Park, which has restrooms, a pavilion with grills, and even a gazebo. The exceptionally well-managed watershed area contains a variety of trees, including hemlock, beech, oak, maple, hickory, basswood, and white, red, and scotch pine. In addition, if you care to fish, the lake has salmon, trout, and panfish. Or try your hand at birdwatching. You may see kingfishers, herons, ospreys, as well as bald eagles near the water. The relatively undisturbed forest along the trail is ideal habitat for several woodpecker species. Also, the narrow lake and forested shoreline create excellent sighting opportunities for spring and autumn migrating warblers and other songbirds.

Trail Directions

- From the parking area, head south past the gate. The trail, an abandoned town road, meanders back and forth through oak, maple, tulip poplar, and conifer trees, but is never far from the lake. See if you can spot the old cottage foundations along the way.
- At the end of the lake, the trail turns left (E) onto gravel.
- At the bench you have a choice. You can continue straight and soon arrive at another gated trail entrance off of Canadice Lake Road, or you can turn right to explore a circle trail with a bench in the center. Off the circle is another trail that also takes you to Canadice Lake Road.

Date Bicycled: ____________

Notes:

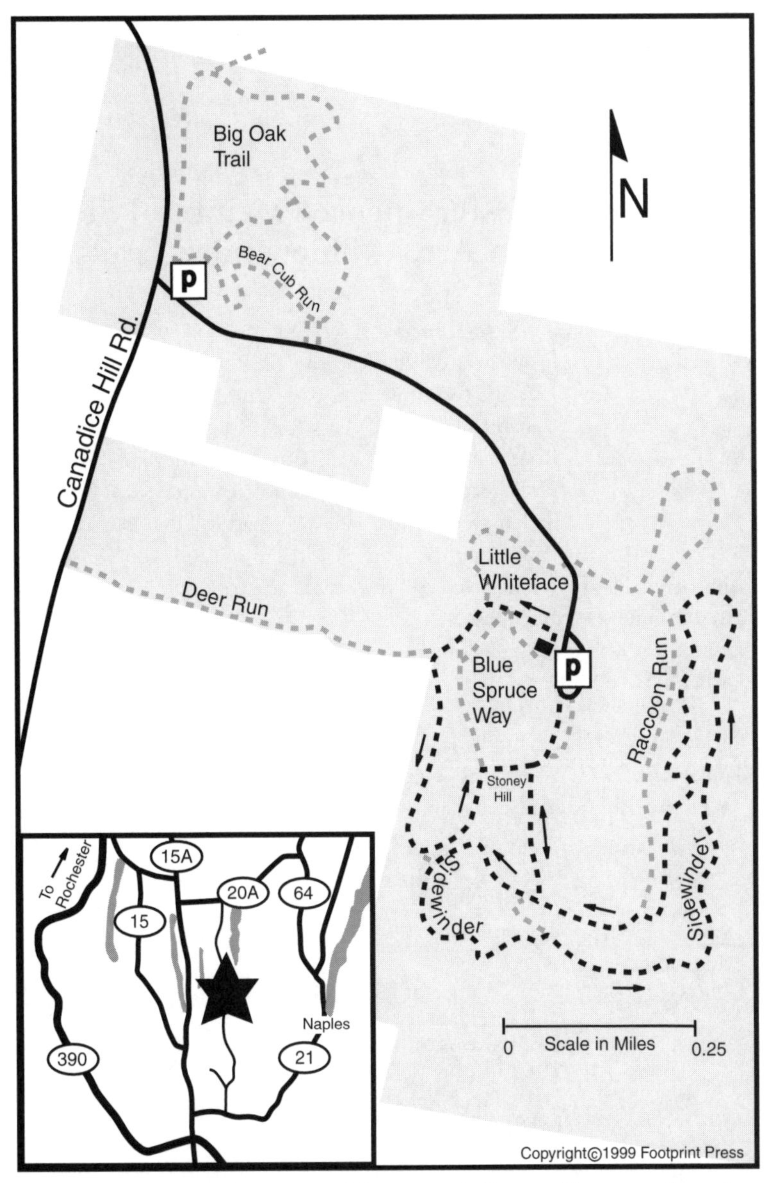

Harriet Hollister Spencer Memorial State Recreation Area
Sidewinder Trail

19.
Harriet Hollister Spencer Memorial State Recreation Area – Sidewinder Trail

Location: South of Honeoye Lake, Ontario County

Directions: From Route 390, head east on Route 20A through Livonia. Continue east, past Route 15A. Turn south on Canadice Hill Road. Pass Ross Road. Canadice Hill Road will turn to gravel. Turn left at the sign "Harriet Hollister Spencer Memorial Recreation Area." Pass a parking area on the left. The road will end in a loop. Park along the road, near the stone and wood lean-to.

Alternative Parking: The paved parking area at the park entrance

Hiking Time: 1.75 hours

Length: 3.3 mile loop

Difficulty:

Surface: Dirt trail

Trail Markings: Some cross-country ski trail signs (blue squares, black diamonds) and some brown-and-yellow trail name signs

Uses: 

Dogs: OK on leash

Admission: Free

Contact: N.Y.S. Office of Parks, Recreation, and Historic Preservation
Stony Brook State Park
10820 Route 36 South
Dansville, NY 14437
(716) 335-8111

The area high in the hills, between Canadice Lake and Honeoye Lake, is treasured by cross-country skiers because it often has snow when the surrounding area doesn't. The trails in this park are constructed, maintained, and groomed in winter by volunteers from the N.Y.S. Section V Ski League.

Honeoye Lake as seen from Harriet Hollister.

As you drive into Harriet Hollister Spencer Memorial State Recreation Area, you'll pass some metal guardrails on the left. Stop in this area to enjoy a grand view of Honeoye Lake in the valley. A bench is available to sit and savor the view. It's labeled "a favorite place of Todd Ewers." The park road is blocked during winter and becomes Overlook Trail – part of the cross-country ski network.

Within the woods you'll follow 8-feet-wide dirt trails. Sometimes narrow trails veer off as shortcuts or deer paths, but stay on the wide trails.

Bed & Breakfast:	The Greenwoods B&B Inn, 8136 Quayle Road, Honeoye, (716) 229-2111
Campground:	Holiday Hill Campground, 7818 Marvin Hill Road, Springwater, (716) 669-2600

Trail Directions

- Walk northwest with your back to the opening of the lean-to.
- Continue straight until the mowed area ends. Then turn left onto the dirt trail and head uphill.

- Continue straight past two trails to the left.
- At the "T," turn left and continue uphill. (Right is Little Whiteface Trail, which winds back to the park road.)
- At the "Y," bear right, uphill.
- Soon reach another "Y." Bear left (S). (Right is Deer Run Trail to Canadice Hill Road.)
- Pass a small trail to the left. Stay on the wide trail.
- Pass a small trail on the right. Stay on the wide trail.
- The trail will bend left.
- Reach a trail junction and turn right on Stony Hill Trail, heading downhill.
- At the next junction, turn right.
- Reach a "T" with a black diamond sign and turn right.
- Bear left at a "Y" to stay on the wide trail. (To the right is a small, yellow blazed connector trail.)
- Pass a caution sign as a long downhill begins.
- The trail sidewinds like a snake traveling through the forest.
- Several small trails cross the main trail.
- Bear right as the connector trail comes in from the left.
- Continue sidewinding on the wide trail.
- Eventually reach a "T" and turn left.
- At the next intersection (with a black diamond sign) turn right.
- Reach a "T" and follow the Raccoon Run sign, turning right.
- Bear left at the next junction.
- Follow the park road back to the lean-to.

Date Bicycled: ____________

Notes:

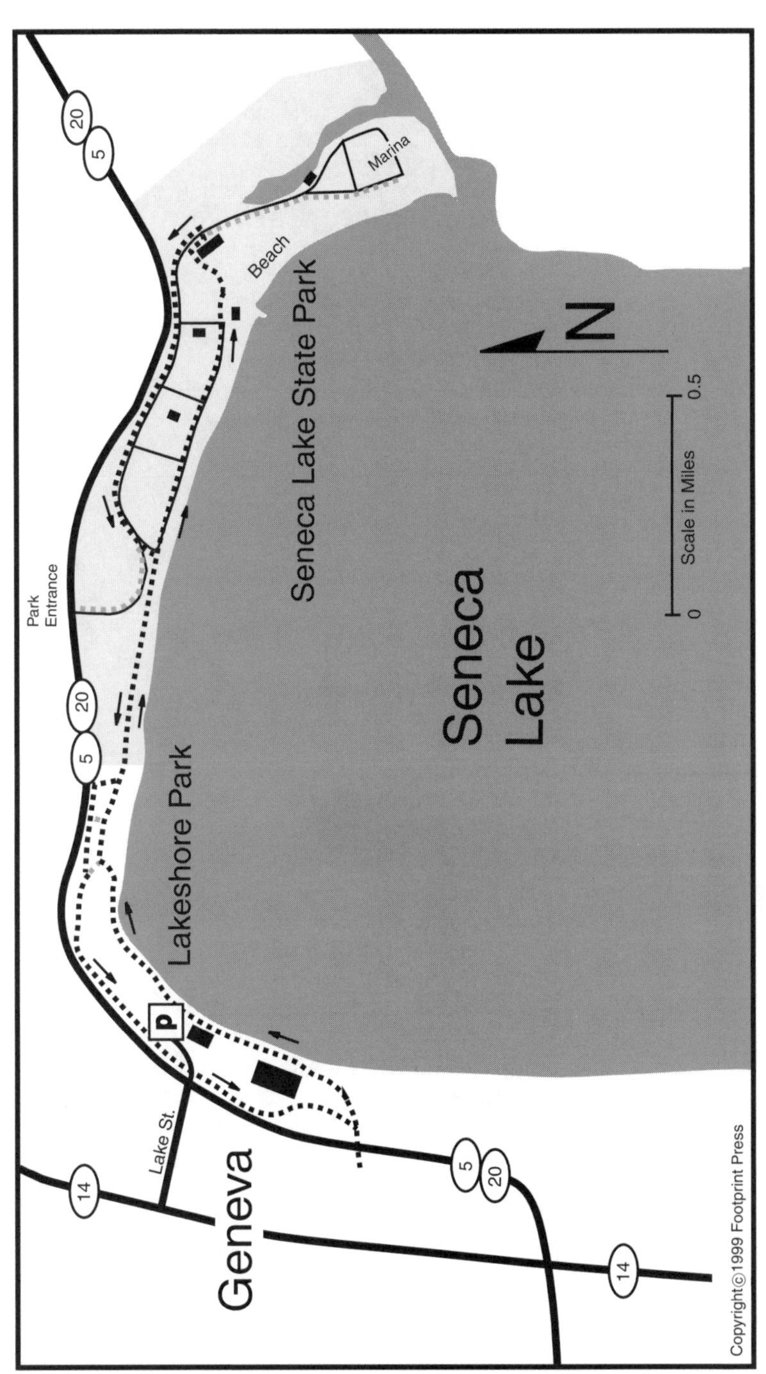

Lakeshore Park / Seneca Lake State Park

20.
Lakeshore Park / Seneca Lake State Park

Location: North end of Seneca Lake in Geneva, Ontario County

Directions: From Route 5 & 20, turn east on Lake Street, into the visitor center parking lot in Lakeshore Park.

Alternative Parking: Parking is available in Seneca Lake State Park. (There is a $4 per vehicle entrance fee.)

Hiking Time: 4.5 hours

Biking Time: 1 hour

Length: 9 mile loop

Difficulty:

Surface: Paved

Trail Markings: ½-mile markings along the lakeshore trail

Uses:    

Dogs: OK on leash

Admission: Free

Contacts: Seneca Lake State Park
1 Lakefront Drive
Geneva, NY 14456
(315) 789-2331

Geneva Area Chamber of Commerce
35 Lakefront Drive, P.O. Box 587
Geneva, NY 14456
(315) 789-1776
http://www.genevany

Ontario County Tourism Bureau
Five Lakes Suite
20 Ontario Street
Canandaigua, NY 14424
(800) 654-9798
http://www.ontariony.com

Seneca Lake is named after the Seneca Indian Nation, one of the Six Nations of the Iroquois Confederacy. The Senecas inhabited these shores long before white settlers arrived.

Seneca Lake is 36 miles long and 632 feet deep at its deepest spot, which makes it the deepest and second longest of the eleven Finger Lakes (Cayuga Lake is 38 miles long). Holding more than four trillion gallons of water, Seneca Lake is the largest Finger Lake. Because of its volume, Seneca Lake rarely freezes in winter. The water moderates the temperature of the surrounding land and makes the area prime for vineyards and orchards.

Seneca Lake State Park was brush, trees, and marsh until 1922, when the city of Geneva developed it into a park. Title was passed to New York State in 1957.

The route described incorporates the paths through Lakeshore Park and Seneca Lake State Park. You'll walk or ride along the lakeshore, shaded by large willow trees. Bring a picnic, there's plenty of picnic tables and grills to enjoy a lake-side meal. The entire route is paved, but sections in Seneca Lake State Park are somewhat rough for in-line skating.

Bed & Breakfasts:	The LaFayette B&B, 107 LaFayette Avenue, Geneva, (315) 781-0068
	Virginia Deane's B&B, 168 Hamilton Street, Geneva, (315) 789-6152
	Belhurst Castle, Route 14 South, Geneva, (315) 781-0201
Bike Shop:	Geneva Bicycle Center, 489 Exchange Street, Geneva, (315) 789-5922
Boat Tour:	Seneca Cruise Company, 212 High Street, Geneva, (315) 789-1822
Campgrounds:	Cheerful Valley Campgrounds, Route 14, north of Geneva, (315) 781-1222
	Junius Ponds Cabins & Campground, Townline Road, Phelps, (315) 781-5120
Ice Cream:	Carvel, 350 Hamilton Street, Geneva, (800) 924-8865
	Mr. Twistee, 758 Pre-Emption Road, Geneva, (315) 781-0858

Trail Directions

• From the Lakeshore Park parking lot head west along the paved trail beside Route 5 and 20, heading back toward Geneva.

- Cross Lake Street at the entrance to the park.
- Cross Castle Street.
- Ride in front of Ramada Inn.
- Cross the entrance to Ramada Inn.
- At the next intersection, turn left and follow the brick path along the lakeshore. (The trail to the right goes through a tunnel and dead-ends.)
- Pass a small gravel segment.
- Ride behind Ramada Inn.
- Continue close to the water.
- Ride behind the visitor center. It has a snack bar.
- Pass a boat ramp as you cut through the Lakeshore Park parking lot.
- At the far end of the parking lot cut over to the bike path. This is the original Route 5 and 20 which often got washed out from high water in Seneca Lake.
- At the next intersection, continue straight to stay near the water.
- Continue straight past two trails to the left.
- Pass a barrier into Seneca Lake State Park.
- Continue along the lake, over 5 speed bumps and past picnic shelter #2.
- Turn left to ride around the park office/bathhouse building. (Restrooms are available here.)
- Ride in front of the park office/bathhouse building and turn left onto the park road. (A right goes to a dead-end at the marina.)
- The road bends left and passes the side road to picnic shelter #2. Continue on the road.
- As you approach the guardhouse, turn left on a short gravel path then an immediate right to return to the Old Route 5 and 20 bike path.
- Cross 5 speed bumps and then the barrier.
- Turn right at the first intersection.
- Bear right past several intersecting trails until you reach the Lakeshore Park parking lot.

Date Bicycled: ______________
Notes:

Rides in Yates, Wayne, & Seneca Counties

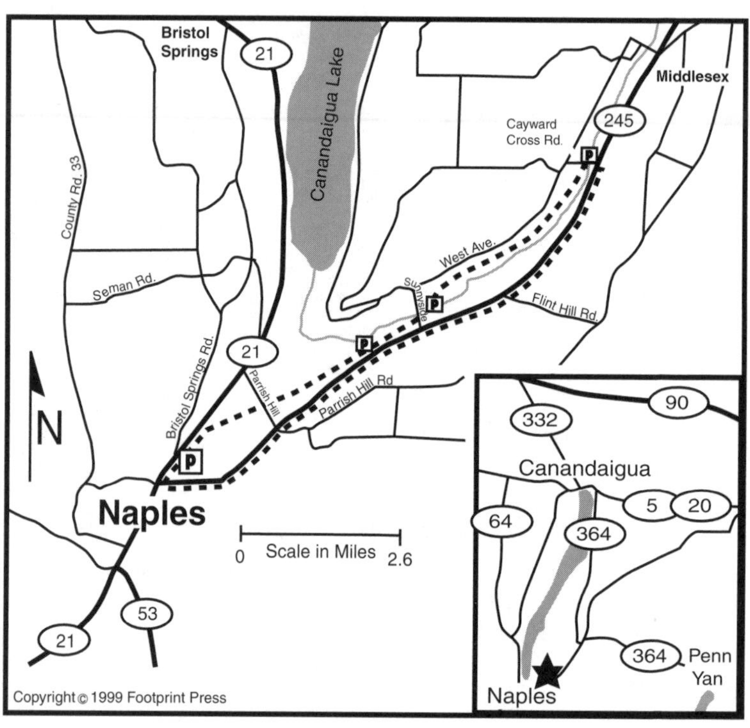

Middlesex Valley Rail Trail

21.
Middlesex Valley Rail Trail

Location: Naples, Yates County

Directions: Follow Route 21 along the west side of Canandaigua Lake. Just north of Naples there will be a large, dirt, pull-off area along Route 21, past the intersection of County Road 12

Alternative Parking: Route 245, Hi-Tor Management Area – West River Unit (boat launch)
Sunnyside Road off Route 245, West River Fishing Access Trail
Cayward Cross Road, off Route 245

Riding Time: 1 hour

Length: 6.8 miles one way (If you return on roads, the round trip is 14.6 miles)

Difficulty:

Surface: Mowed grass

Trail Markings: None

Uses: 

Dogs: OK on leash

Admission: Free

Contacts: N. Y. S. Department of Environmental Conservation
6274 Avon-Lima Road
Avon, NY 14414
(716) 226-2466
http://www.dec.state.ny.us

The official name of this trail is the Lehigh Valley Trail. However, because other sections of the Lehigh are open for biking and hiking, we've called it by its historical name. Don't let the fact that this is an old rail bed fool you into thinking it's an easy ride. As you pedal north, you don't notice a grade. But the pedaling is tough as the trail goes steadily uphill. This ride is well worth the effort, however, because you'll find scenery that you won't see on any other rail trail. You'll ride through Middlesex Valley with the tower-

Riding in Naples Valley along the Middlesex Valley Rail Trail.

ing hills of Naples on either side. Most of the rail bed is a raised platform through a wetland. But, because it passes through wetlands, it may be impassable in wet weather. Along the way are waterfowl nesting boxes; and about 1 mile south of Cayward Cross Road is a blue heron rookery. Please be quiet and don't disturb the birds.

The Middlesex Valley Railroad first provided service between Naples and Stanley in 1892. The line was later extended to Geneva. In 1895, the rail line was purchased by the Lehigh Valley Railroad. Service continued until 1970, when the line was abandoned due to competition from trucks and cars for the freight of coal, building materials, farm equipment, apples, grapes, beans, etc. Most of the land reverted to private ownership. This portion of the rail trail is owned by New York State as part of the Hi-Tor Game Management Area. It is a public hunting ground, so avoid bicycling during hunting season.

Bed & Breakfasts: Lakeview Farm B&B, 4761 Route 364, Rushville, (716) 554-6973

Naples Valley B&B, 7161 County Road 12, Naples, (800) 577-6331

	Vagabond Inn, 3300 Sliter Road, Naples, (716) 554-6271
	Victoriana B&B, 2687 West Main Street, Gorham, (716) 526-4531
Campground:	Flint Hill Campgrounds, Middlesex, (716) 554-3567

Distance between major roads:

Route 21 to Parish Hill	1.2 miles
Parish Hill to Sunnyside	2.6 miles
Sunnyside to Cayward Cross	3.0 miles

Trail Directions

- Head toward the yellow metal gate and stop sign onto a 12-foot-wide, mowed-grass path.
- Cross the first of many wooden bridges over a creek.
- Emerge from the woods to a vineyard, then a field on your right. The Naples hills tower above as a backdrop to the fields.
- Continue parallel to the creek.
- Cross the second wooden bridge. The D.E.C. repaired these bridges.
- Pass a yellow metal gate then cross Parish Hill Road.
- Pass another yellow metal gate and ride through a raised bed over wetlands.
- Cross the third wooden bridge. Here are some short sections of ballast stone.
- Cross the fourth-wooden bridge, then a few more short sections of ballast.
- The trail now runs parallel to a road.
- Cross the fifth wooden bridge.
- Pass through a backyard of farm animals. This is home to a horse, donkey, lamb, and goat as well as many ducks, geese, guinea fowl, turkeys, chickens, and rabbits. The front of this home is a roadside farm stand where produce, tarts, pies, breads, snacks, and drinks are sold.
- Pass through another yellow gate into the parking area and boat launch for Hi-Tor Management Area – West River Unit.
- Head toward the first yellow gate.
- Pass more yellow gates.
- Pass the West River Fishing Access site. The West River is on your left. Across the river is the legendary site of the first Seneca Indian village, Nundawao.

- Cross Sunnyside Road. You've ridden 3.8 miles so far.
- Pass yellow gates.
- Cross a long wooden bridge where the waters fork. Trailers are on the left, and a beaver dam and dens are on the right.
- Cross the seventh wooden bridge. Enjoy wetlands on both sides of the path.
- Continue on a long stretch through a wooded area.
- The land again turns to wetlands, this time with clumps of wild daylilies along the shore.
- The path ends at the yellow gates at Cayward Cross Road. From here you have two options. One is to turn around and follow the rail trail back to the start. The other is to follow the roads back. The roads have good paved shoulders and are predominately downhill. Turn right (E) onto Cayward Cross Road, right onto Route 245, then right again when the road ends at Route 21. This takes you back to the start. Along the way, pass an old cemetery and a roadside farm stand.

Date Bicycled: ______________

Notes:

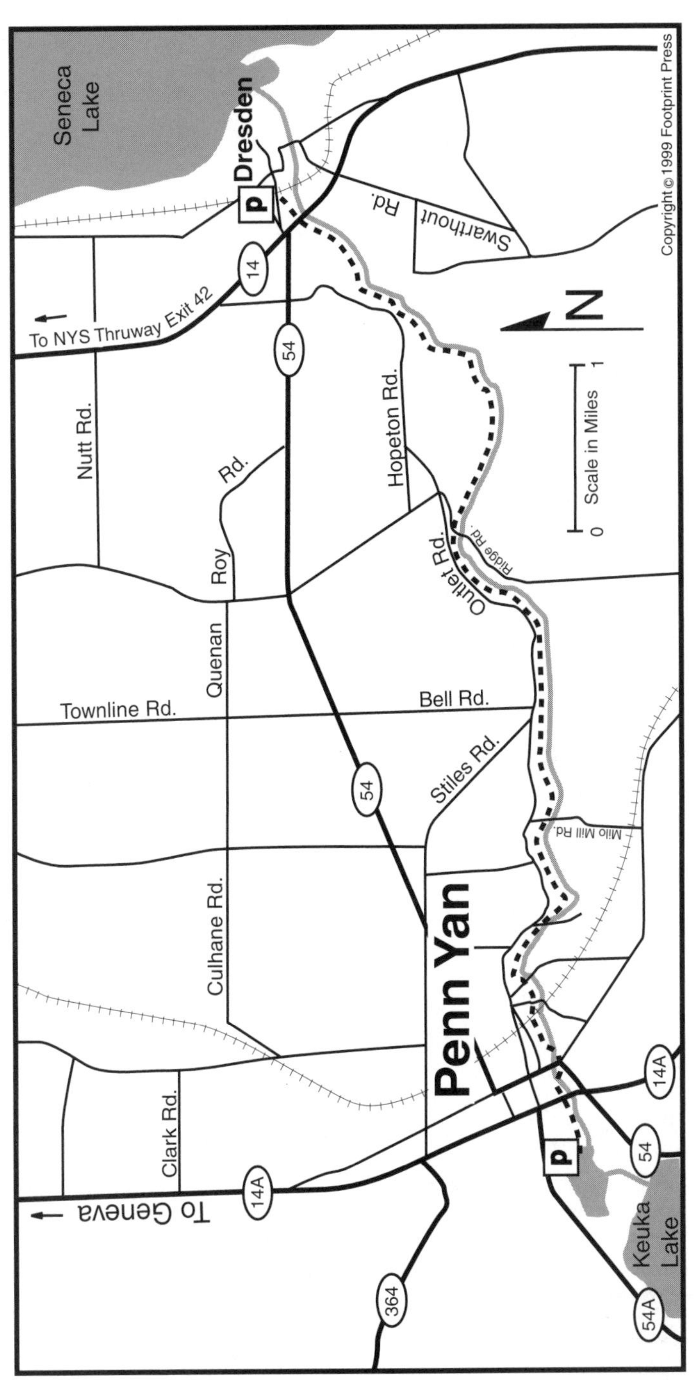

Keuka Lake Outlet Trail

22.
Keuka Lake Outlet Trail

Location: Dresden to Penn Yan, Yates County

Directions: From Route 14 south along the west side of Seneca Lake, turn left (E) at Route 54 heading toward Main Street, Dresden. There is a Citgo gas station and the Crossroads Ice Cream Shop at the corner. At the Crossroads Ice Cream Shop, take an immediate right onto Seneca Street. Parking is on your right just before the railroad tracks.

Alternative Parking: Elm Street (Route 54A), Penn Yan, Marsh Development Project – Little League Baseball

Riding Time: 1.25 hours

Length: 7.5 miles one way

Difficulty:

Surface: Dirt (western end is paved)

Trail Markings: Green-and-white metal "Trail" signs

Uses:

Dogs: OK on leash

Admission: Free

Contact: Friends of the Finger Lakes Outlet
P.O. Box 231
Penn Yan, NY 14527

The strip of land you will be biking from Seneca Lake to Keuka Lake is steeped in history. You'll see the evidence of places and events from several bygone eras as you pedal westward.

In the middle of the nineteenth century, two fingers of water connected the 274-foot drop between Keuka and Seneca Lakes, they were, the outlet to power mills and the Crooked Lake Canal for boat traffic. A dam and guardhouse in Penn Yan controlled the water flow to both. The outlet, which still carries water from one lake to the next, was formed by a ground fault in the Tully limestone allowing water to run between the two lakes.

Along its banks you'll see remnants of the many mills that once harnessed the waterpower.

The first white settlers arrived in this area around 1788, attracted by the reliable water source at the outlet. In 1789, Seneca Mill was built along the raging waters of Keuka Lake Outlet to grind flour with a 26-foot, overshot flywheel. From then until 1827, a small religious group called the Society of Universal Friends built 12 dams and many mills that helped make the area a thriving community. The mills and shops produced flour (gristmills), lumber (sawmills), tool handles, linseed oil, plaster, and liquor (distilleries). There were two triphammer forges, eight fulling and carding mills, tanneries, and weavers making cotton and wool cloth. By 1835, 30 to 40 mills were in operation. But, by 1900, only 5 mills remained, mainly making paper from straw. The last water-turbine mill ceased operation in 1968.

Keuka Lake Outlet rushes past abandoned mills and factories.

In 1833, New York State opened the Crooked Lake Canal to span the 6 miles between the two lakes and move farm products to eastern markets. The canal was 4 feet deep and had 28 wooden locks. It took a vessel 6 hours to journey through the canal. As business boomed in the mills, the state widened and deepened the canal and replaced the wooden locks with stone. But, the canal lost money every year of its 44-year history, so in

1877, the state auctioned off all of the machinery and stone. Only the towpath remained.

In 1844, a railroad was built on the towpath. Initially operated by the Penn Yan and New York Railway Company, it eventually became part of the New York Central System. Railway men called it the "Corkscrew Railway" because of its countless twists and turns. The line operated until 1972, when the tracks were washed out by the flood from Hurricane Agnes.

A local group interested in recreational use of the ravine convinced the town of Penn Yan to buy the property in 1981. Since then, it has been developed and maintained by a volunteer group called the Friends of the Outlet. Trail signs and outhouses were recently added along the route.

Reference Guides: Purchase an illustrated guide to the Keuka Lake Outlet for $1.00 from the Yates County Historian, 110 Court Street, Penn Yan, NY 14527. A packet of information on the history of the mill sites, canal, and railroad of the Keuka Lake Outlet is available for $3.00 at stores in Penn Yan.

Bed & Breakfasts:	Finton's Landing B&B, 661 East Lake Road, Penn Yan, (315) 536-3146
	Fox Inn, 158 Main Street, Penn Yan, (800) 901-7997
	Keuka Overlook, 5777 Old Bath Road, Dundee, (607) 292-6877
	Merrit Hill Manor, 2756 Coates Road, Penn Yan, (315) 536-7682
	Trimmer House B&B, 145 East Main Street, Penn Yan, (800) 968-8735
	Tudor Hall B&B, 762 East Bluff Drive, Penn Yan, (315) 536-9962
	The Wagener Estate, 351 Elm Street, Penn Yan, (315) 536-4591
Bike Rental:	Crossroads Ice Cream Shop, Dresden, (315) 531-5311, (call for reservations)
Bike Shop:	Weaver's Bicycle Shop, Route 14A, Penn Yan (315) 536-3012

Campground: Wigwam Keuka Lake Campground, 3324 Esperanza Road, Bluff Point, (315) 536-6352

Ice Cream: Crossroads Ice Cream Shop, Dresden, (315) 531-5311

Distances between major roads:	
Seneca Street to Ridge Road	2.6 miles
Ridge Road to Milo Mill Road	1.8 miles
Milo Mill Road to Fox Mill Road	1.1 miles
Fox Mill Road to Cherry Street	0.1 mile
Cherry Street to Main Street	0.9 mile
Main Street to Route 54A	1.0 mile

Trail Directions

- The trail leads downhill from the back-right corner of the Dresden parking lot, heading west.
- Cross under the Route 14 bridge. The land you're on used to be the Dresden Mill Pond.
- The wetland to your right (north of the trail) is the old Crooked Lake Canal.
- Cross two wooden bridges
- Notice the steep cliffs on both sides. Here where the canal and outlet are close together was the location of Lock 3. Watch for the cement and rebar millstone.
- Cross a dirt road. This was Hopeton Road, which connected Geneva to Bath through the town of Hopeton in the 1790s. To your left you can still see remnants of the iron-pony, truss bridge over the outlet. The bridge was built in 1840, and rests on stone abutments. This area was once a community of mills.
- Hopeton Grist Mill was located just beyond the dirt road on the left. Nothing remains of it today.
- On your left is a pleasant rest area with large rocks that you can sit on along the water.
- Across the outlet, Bruces Gully cascades water over three waterfalls to join the outlet. Eventually the Friends of the Outlet plan to build a hiking trail through the gully. The dark gray rock, which peels in thin layers, is Genesee shale.
- Pass a cement pillar on your right.The big "W" on the pillar signaled the train conductor to blow his whistle.
- At the two-mile point are the remains of the J.T. Baker Chemical

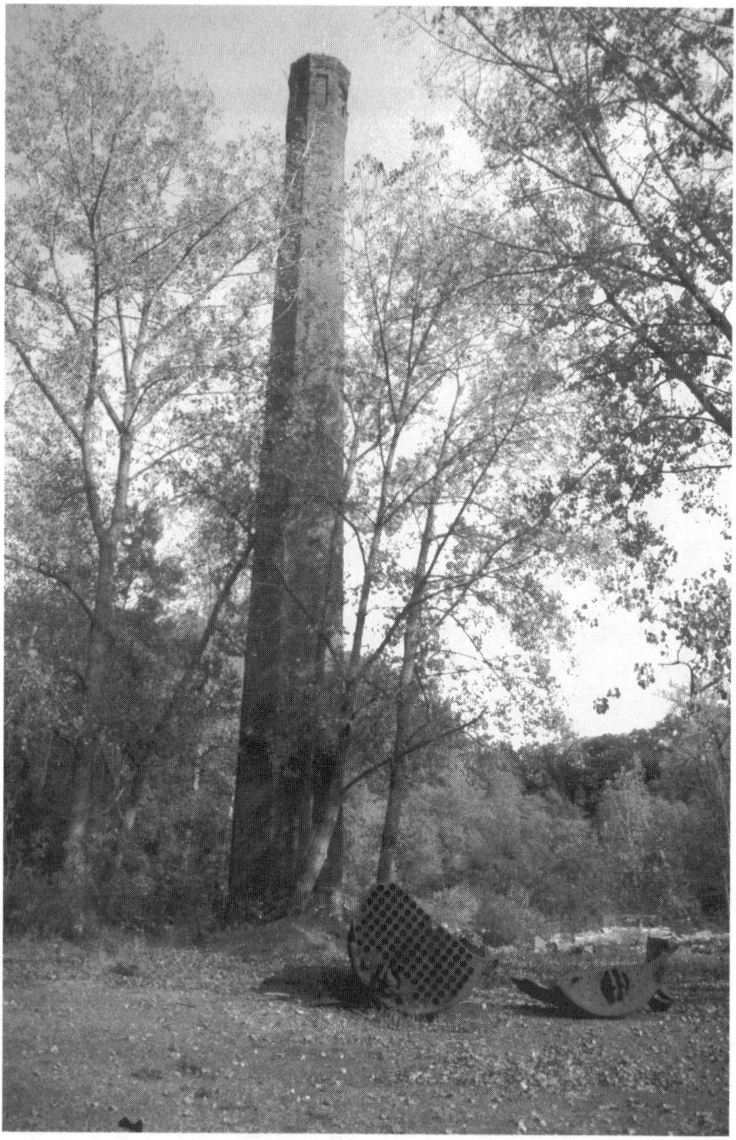

Remains of a papermill from 1890.

Company, manufacturers of the pesticide carbine bisulfide until 1968. At one time, this was also the site of a gristmill and several paper mills.

- Here you'll see your first waterfall. The top step of the falls was the old dam, constructed in 1827, and the last of the 12 dams to be built along the outlet. Both Cascade Mill and Mallory's Mill used the water that was held back by this dam.
- Follow the wide gravel path through the building area.
- Pass old Kelly Tire buildings. The Friends of the Outlet recently renovated these buildings into the Alfred Jensen Memorial Visitor Center. It's a good place to stop if you need a restroom.
- Follow the green-and-white trail signs as the trail branches to the left.
- Cross the paved Ridge Road. In 1805 May's Mills stood at this site. It had a gristmill, a sawmill, and a post office. In the 1820s this area was home to a cotton factory, then a distillery.
- Continue along the outlet. Outlet Road parallels close to the trail.
- Just over a culvert is another cement post displaying a "W," then another cement marker with "D3," which told the conductor that Dresden was 3 miles away. This means that you're almost halfway to Penn Yan.
- Pass a parking lot off Outlet Road. The brick remnants on the right were once a factory that turned rags into paper.
- Look for the large rock between the bike path and the outlet. A plaque on the side facing the outlet commemorates John Sheridan, a lawyer who negotiated the purchase of land for the Keuka Lake Outlet Preservation Area. The stone remnants across the outlet were once a forge. At one time a road crossed over the dam at this spot. Seneca Mill, the first mill site, was located at this falls, the largest falls on the outlet.
- On your right (away from the outlet) is a stone wall with a large round opening. This used to house a pipe to vent train smoke out of the valley.
- The machinery that remains at the top of the dam controlled water flow through a sluiceway. The original Friends Mill, a complex of paper and grist mills, was here.
- The trail bears right through Lock 17, which was the downstream end of a series of four locks needed to maneuver the elevation drop.
- You're now biking in a ravine of the old canal bed. In May, this segment of trail is lined with trillium. It's also an active beaver area.
- Pass another cement whistle sign on the right.
- The cement wall in the water is the end of a race from Milo Mills. The

stagnant water on the left is the raceway. From here to Penn Yan was the most industrialized section of the outlet.

- A large brick chimney towers over the remains of a paper mill, built in 1890, burned in 1910, and then rebuilt. You can still see the 17-foot flywheel that used 2 miles of hemp cable and was run by a steam engine. The machinery was manufactured at the Rochester Foundry at Brown's Race.
- Cross Milo Mill Road.
- Cross a bridge over a wood-lined sluice. This sluice used to carry water to Shutt's Mill, which dates back to about 1850.
- A small sidepath immediately to the left leads to the ruins of Shutt's Mill. You can still see the stone vats from this paper mill, which manufactured wallboard. Shutt's Mill burned in 1933. The first mill at this site was a sawmill built in 1812. It was followed by a wool mill, a gristmill, and a fulling mill. Beware of the poison ivy in the area.
- The waterfall on the far side of the outlet, just before a road and bridge, is outflow from the municipal sewage plant.
- Cross a road. Dibbles Mill used to make wooden wheels in this area.
- The green shed across the road on the right was a blacksmith shop from canal times (around 1838). The blacksmith specialized in shoeing mules.
- Cross paved Fox Mill Road. If you take a left on Fox Mill Road, then a quick right toward the outlet, you'll find remains from the Fox Mill that manufactured straw paper. The stone for the walls was moved here from the dismantled locks of Crooked Lake Canal around 1865.
- Pass a sign for St. John's Mill. Other than the sign, there's nothing to see. The mill used to be across the outlet.
- Cross paved Cherry Street, at 5.5 miles.
- The trail becomes paved.
- Pass under a railroad trestle called "High Bridge." It was originally built of wood in 1850 and was rebuilt in 1890.
- The large circular hollow just after the trestle was once a turntable for the train.
- Pass signs for an exercise trail. After the chin-up bars on the right, a small path leads left to another cement railroad marker "D6," indicating 6 miles from Dresden.
- Reach the wooden bridge, which served as a railroad trestle to Birkett Mills in 1824. Birkett Mills took their water turbines out in 1947.
- Pass under the Main Street (Penn Yan) bridge, built from canal stone in 1884. This area used to have the guardhouse for the canal. The dam on the right is used to control water level in Keuka Lake. The brown

building you can see was a grain warehouse. At one time this section of trail was home to several woodworking factories, a cooperage, and a sash-and-blind factory.

- Pass through a park.
- Cross the pedestrian bridge over the outlet.
- Continue through Penn Yan Recreation Complex on the paved path. You pass restrooms, a boat launch, tennis courts, and a small play ground.
- Cross another wooden bridge over Sucker Brook.
- Pass through the athletic fields to the parking lot in Marsh Development Project on Route 54A.
- The trail ends here. You can turn around and retrace your path.

Date Bicycled: ______________

Notes:

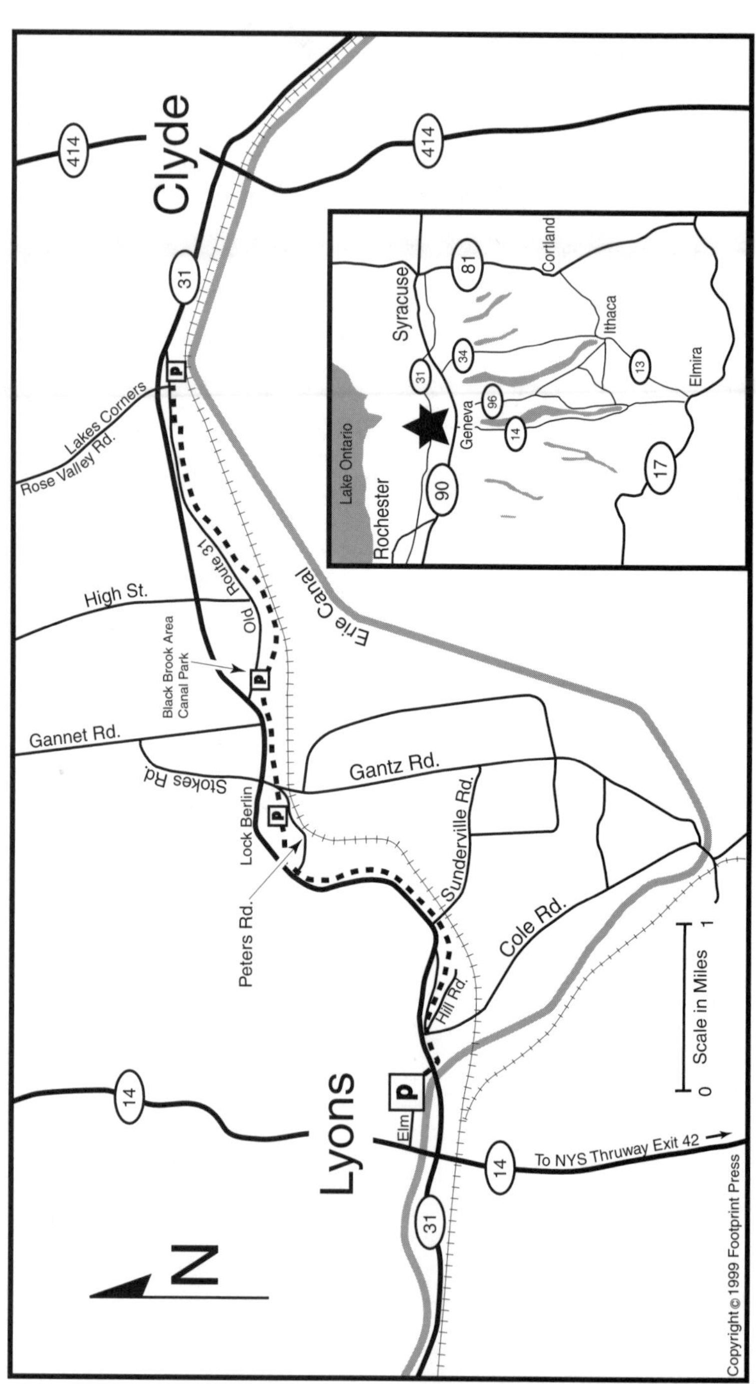

Canal Park Trailway

23.
Canal Park Trailway

Location: Lyons to Clyde, Wayne County
Directions: Head north through Lyons on Route 14, over the Erie Canal. Turn right on Elm Street. Drive until the road ends, past the Little League Field. Park in the Village of Lyon's Public Works Department parking area.
Alternative Parking: At road crossings
The intersection of Route 31 and Old Route 31
Riding Time: 1 hour
Length: 5.8 miles one way
Difficulty:
Surface: Mowed-grass path
Trail Markings: 2-by 3-foot, white, blue, and red signs
Uses:
Dogs: OK on leash
Admission: Free
Contact: Wayne County Planning Department
9 Pearl Street
Lyons, NY 14489
(315) 946-5919

Follow history back in time as you pedal from the existing Erie Canal to the original Clinton's Ditch of 1817, and the enlarged Erie Canal of the 1850s. Along the way pass stone locks, long abandoned. On one trip we saw flocks of wild turkey and a beaver repairing his den. Locals say the old canal waters are a great fishing spot for bass and sunfish.

The Erie Canal, dubiously called "Clinton's Ditch," opened for operation in 1825. It was a 40-foot-wide water channel with locks 90 feet long and 15 feet wide. Boats with loads up to 75 tons could navigate the waters. By 1840, a greater capacity was needed because commerce along the canal boomed, and the canal was enlarged to 70 feet wide. Locks increased to 110 feet long and 18 feet wide, allowing cargoes up to 200 tons.

By 1909, the canal was over capacity again. This time, the canal was rerouted in places as it was enlarged. The name was changed to reflect its growing purpose. The new-and-improved Barge Canal opened in 1918, allowing cargoes of 3,000 tons to pass through its 45-foot-wide locks. The opening of the Saint Lawrence Seaway eliminated the need to transfer goods to barges and rendered the canal obsolete. The name was changed back to its historic one: the Erie Canal.

Bed & Breakfasts:	Peppermint Cottage B&B, 336 Pleasant Valley Road, Lyons, (315) 946-4811
	Roselawne B&B, 101 Broad Street, Lyons, (315) 946-4218
Campground:	Nor-Win Farm & Campsite, 2921 Pilgrimport Road, Lyons, (315) 946-4436

Distances between major roads:	
Route 14 to Hill Road	0.7 mile
Hill Road to Sunderville Road	0.7 mile
Sunderville Road to Peters Road	1.0 mile
Peters Road to Gansz Road	0.6 mile
Gansz Road to Black Brook Area Canal Park	0.7 mile
Black Brook Area Canal Park to Route 31	2.1 miles

Trail Directions

- From the sign saying "Canal Park Trailway" at the end of Elm Street, Lyons, head east through the backyard of a gray apartment complex. The current Erie Canal is to your right.
- Ride under the Route 31 bridge. Beware of a small washout under the bridge.
- The trail winds left, away from the canal to parallel Route 31.
- Stay on the grass path that leads over a pedestrian bridge to cross a small creek.
- Continue uphill parallel to Route 31.
- Ride across Cross Road.
- Ride on Old Route 31 road for a short distance.
- At the intersection of Hill Road, continue straight on the grass path between Old Route 31 and Hill Road.
- Pass an old stone bridge abutment. Clinton's Ditch is on your left.
- Cross Sunderville Road. Clinton's Ditch continues to be on your left.

- Cross Peter's Road.
- Pass an abandoned, stone, double lock. A park with picnic tables and grills is at the lock (Berlin Lock).
- Cross Gansz Road. The canal is dammed at this point and becomes a trickle in a ditch from here east.
- Cross a small wooden bridge.
- A short side trail to the left goes to stonework around a feeder creek, which is actually half of an original Clinton's Ditch lock rebuilt to form a waste weir.
- A path to the left, across a crooked wooden bridge, leads to Black Brook Area Canal Park. This park has restrooms, a pavilion, picnic tables, grills, and a playground.
- The mowed path ends at a driveway. You can turn around here to head back or turn left onto the driveway, then right (E) onto Old Route 31, and ride 0.9 mile to the junction of Route 31 where parking is available.

Date Bicycled: ______________

Notes:

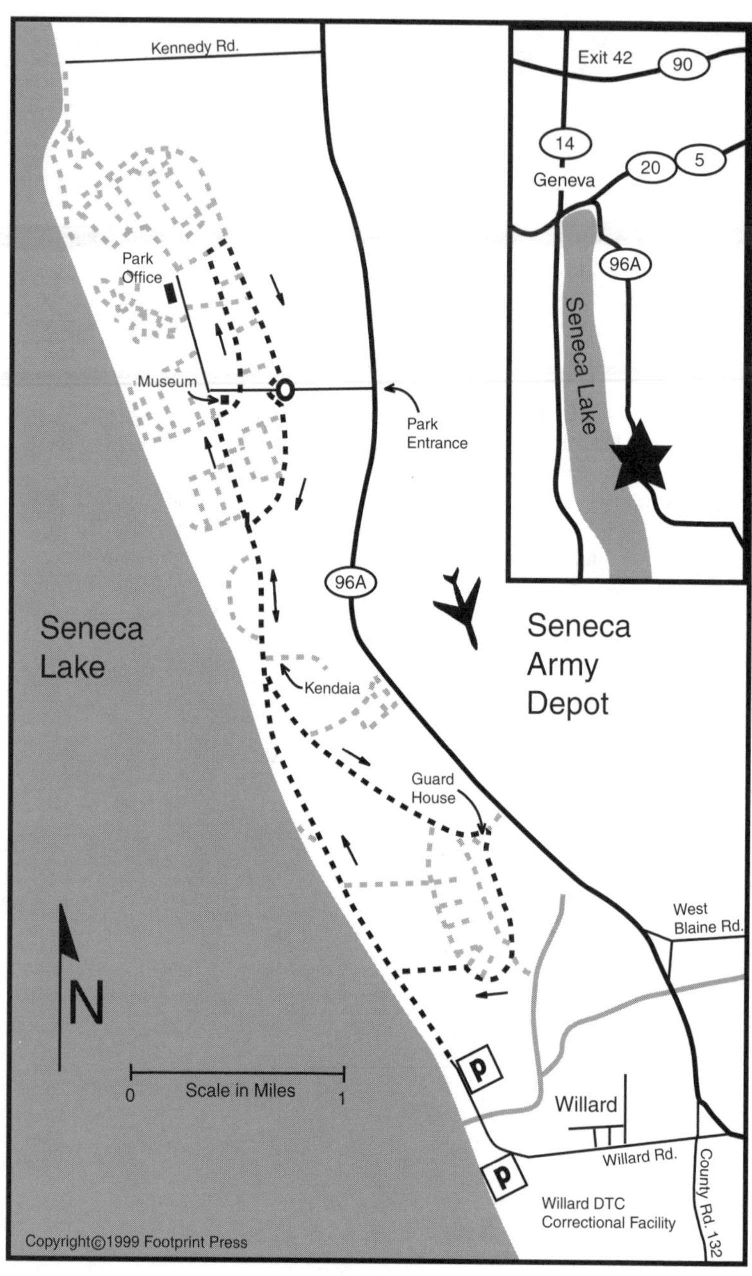

Sampson State Park - Lake Trail

24.
Sampson State Park – Lake Trail

Location: On the east side of Seneca Lake, Seneca County

Directions: Take Route 96A south from Geneva. Pass Sampson State Park. Where Route 96A bends east, bear right on County Road 132. Turn west on Willard Road. Follow Willard Road as it bends right and parallels the shore of Seneca Lake. The parking area is on the right of Willard Road at the barrier.

Alternative Parking: In Sampson State Park (costs $5 per vehicle from Memorial Day to Labor Day)

Biking Time: 2 hours

Length: 9.4 mile loop

Difficulty:

Surface: Old paved roads

Trail Markings: None

Uses:

Dogs: OK on leash

Admission: Free (from Willard entrance)

Contact: Sampson State Park
6096 Route 96A
Romulus, NY 14541
(315) 585-6392

This is a family biking paradise. A network of abandoned roads from the Sampson Naval Training Station provide hours of nooks and crannies to explore. The trails (roads) are paved, but the abandoned ones are being overgrown with weeds and undermined with roots. This combination keeps cars out and means safe bicycling.

The first humans to use this area were nomadic hunters. By the early 1600s, the Seneca Indians had established an agricultural community called Kendaia. This settlement was burned by the Continental Army during the Revolutionary War. After the war, much of the land between Seneca and

Cayuga Lakes was awarded to soldiers as payment for their services. They moved in and established farms where once the Indians thrived.

A century and a half later, with the outbreak of World War II, quiet farm life made way for the second largest navel training station in the country. It was named for a Palmyra resident, Rear Admiral William T. Sampson. After the war, Sampson State College was located on the base to educate returning servicemen. Sampson was used as an airforce base during the Korean War, and became a state park in 1960.

The old drill fields and other cleared lands are slowing growing up in grasses, wildflowers, shrubs, and trees. Some buildings have been removed, but others remain as shells of their former selves. Use your imagination as you ride through this area to conjure up images of the days when the naval base thrived.

Your ride will begin on the Lake Trail, a road of many names. It began as a Seneca Indian trail. While used as a World War II Naval station it was called Mahan Road. This name was changed to Liberator Road when the Air Force managed the area as a training facility. Maps today label it as East Lake Road but it is closed to cars. Lake Trail was resurfaced in 1997. It runs for 1.7 miles from the parking area on Willard Road to Sampson State Park.

Once in the park, your ride will loop around some rarely used back roads and then head south through the abandoned naval complex, reconnecting with Lake Trail. You'll ride through areas of abandoned buildings and have spectacular views of Seneca Lake.

Along Lake Trail you'll find numbered wooden posts that identify trees. In 1998 Boy Scout Jonathan Lanning installed these as his Eagle project. His brochure, which gives the scientific names, descriptions, and uses of each of the following types of trees, is available at the Sampson State Park Office and Recreation Building.

1. Northern White Cedar
2. Eastern Red Cedar
3. Eastern Cottonwood
4. Sugar Maple
5. Basswood
6. Black Locust
7. White Oak
8. Big-toothed Aspen
9. Black Walnut
10. Shagbark Hickory
11. White Ash
12. Red Oak
13. Hop Hornbeam

If you head south to the trailhead in Willard, you'll pass Sampson State Park on the right and the fenced in area of Seneca Army Depot on the left. Watch carefully along the way. The deer herd in Seneca Army Depot includes rare white deer (not technically albino deer). As we drove south, once we spotted 3 deer just inside the fence. One was a normal brown white-tailed deer, one was a grazing white doe, and on the ground rested a white buck with full antlers.

Bike Rental:	Sampson State Park Office and Recreation Building, $5/hour or $20/day
Campground:	Sampson State Park, 6096 Route 96A, Romulus, (315) 585-6392
Ice Cream:	Village Soft Serve, Main Street, Ovid

Trail Directions

- From the Willard Road parking area, head north past large boulders on Lake Trail.
- Pass several trails and old roads intersecting Lake Trail.
- At 0.9 mile, a gravel trail on the left leads down to the shore of Seneca Lake.
- More old roads intersect but continue straight.
- At 1.7 miles pass large boulders and a post in the road.
- Two major roads will be on the right. A sign describing Kendaia is at the second one. Continue straight.
- Pass more roads, a service road, and a maintenance building.
- At 3.1 miles you'll reach a major road intersection. The large, fenced-in, red brick Navy Museum building will be kitty-corner to the right. (To the left is the boat launch.) Turn right.
- Cross the main entrance road.
- Continue straight past road intersections and a log over the road, until the road ends at a "T." Turn right (E).
- At the next intersection turn right (S) and pass a block building on the left.
- Continue straight. At a "Y" bear right.
- At 4.8 miles, reach the traffic circle with a memorial statue. Bear right around the circle to continue straight across.
- Pass more roads. At a "T," turn left (S).
- Pass several roads, including the one with the Kendaia sign.
- At the next "Y," bear left.

An abandoned guardhouse marks the entrance to the Naval Training Station.

- At 7.1 miles, cross a dirt barrier mound.
- Pass several roads. At the old guardhouse, turn right.
- Pass more roads, then a series of abandoned buildings.
- After the buildings there will be a road to the right and a road to the left (into woods). Continue bearing right on the old road until the next road to the left. Take this left and begin heading downhill toward Seneca Lake. Pause to enjoy the view.
- The trail will narrow and turn to dirt for a short distance. Cross a dirt gully before re-joining the paved road.
- At 8.9 miles, reach a "T" and turn left back on the Lake Trail.
- Follow Lake Trail downhill to the parking area.

Date Bicycled: ______________
Notes:

Rides in Schuyler & Tompkins Counties

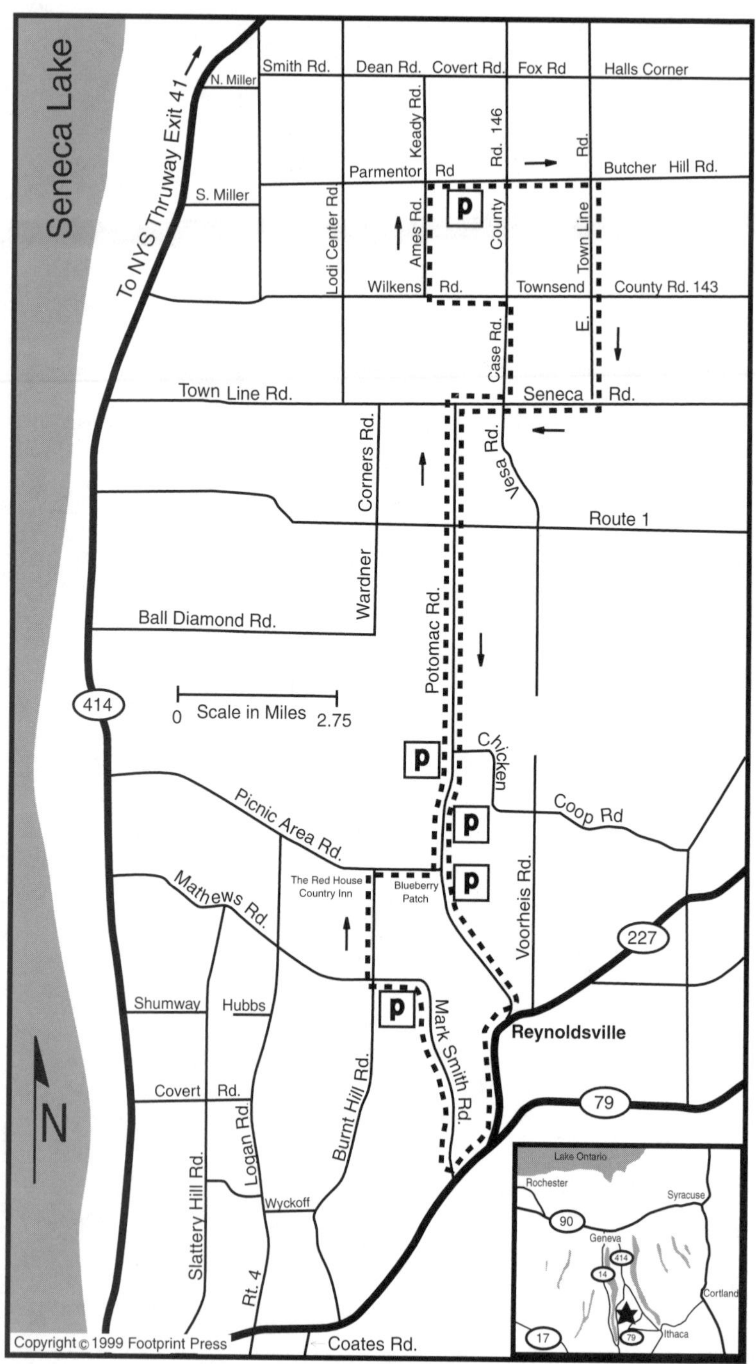

Finger Lakes National Forest Trail

25.
Finger Lakes National Forest Trail

Location: Between Seneca and Cayuga Lakes, Schuyler County
Directions: Take Route 96A south along the eastern side of Seneca Lake, through Ovid and Lodi. Just past Lodi, turn south onto Keady Road. Take the third left onto Parmentor Road. The Interloken Trail parking lot is on the right.
Alternative Parking: Foster Pond parking on Potomac Road
Potomac Group Campground on Potomac Road
Intersection of Potomac Road and Picnic Area Road
South Pasture parking on Mathews Road
Ravine Trail parking on Picnic Area Road
Riding Time: 4.5 hours
Length: 25.1 mile loop
Difficulty:
Surface: Mostly packed dirt roads, some paved roads
Trail Markings: None
Uses:
Dogs: OK on leash
Admission: Free
Contact: Finger Lakes National Forest
5218 State Road 414
Hector, NY 14841-9707
(607) 546-4470

The Finger Lakes National Forest encompasses 16,000 acres of land and has over 30 miles of interconnecting hiking trails. The trails are not open to bicycles. The forest is, however, crisscrossed by a network of single-lane dirt roads that are excellent for biking. These roads are open April 1 through November 30 only. Because the national forest is open to hunting, biking during hunting season is not recommended.

From a bicycle you can explore the deep forests and steep hills of this varied countryside. The forest contains a five-acre blueberry patch. What better treat on any bike excursion than devouring a handful of freshly picked blueberries. August and September are the best months to find ripe blueberries. This forest also offers overnight camping and has a privately owned bed-and-breakfast, making it a perfect weekend getaway. Contact the Finger Lakes National Forest for additional information on camping. Two hiking loops are described in the book *Take A Hike! Family Walks in the Finger Lakes & Genesee Valley Region*.

The area around the Finger Lakes National Forest was originally inhabited by the Iroquois Indians, though little is known of their use of the region. In 1790, the area was divided into 600-acre military lots and distributed among Revolutionary War veterans as payment for their services. These early settlers cleared the land for production of hay and small grains such as buckwheat. As New York City grew, a strong market for these products developed, encouraging more intensive agriculture. The farmers prospered until the middle of the nineteenth century, when a series of unfortunate events occurred: the popularity of motorized transportation in urban centers (reducing the number of horses to be fed), gradual depletion of the soil resource, and competition from midwestern agriculture.

Between 1890 and the Great Depression, over a million acres of farmland were abandoned in south-central New York State. In the 1930s, it was obvious that farmers in many parts of the country could no longer make a living from their exhausted land. Environmental damage worsened as they cultivated the land more and more intensively to make ends meet. Several pieces of legislation were passed, including the Emergency Relief Act of 1933 and the Bankhead-Jones Farm Tenant Act of 1937, to address these problems. A new government agency, the Resettlement Administration, was formed to carry out the new laws. This agency not only directed the relocation of farmers to better land or other jobs but also the purchase of marginal farmland by the federal government.

Between 1938 and 1941, more than 100 farms were purchased in the Finger Lakes National Forest area and administered by the Soil Conservation Service. Because this was done on a willing-seller, willing-buyer basis, the resulting federal ownership resembled a patchwork quilt. The land was named the Hector Land Use Area and was managed to stabilize the soil by planting conifers and developing a grazing program. Individual livestock owners were allowed to graze animals on the pastureland to show how less intensive agriculture could still make productive use of the land.

By the 1950s, many of the objectives of the Hector Land Use Area had been met, and the public was becoming interested in the concept of multiple uses of public land. In 1954, administration responsibilities were transferred to the U.S. Forest Service. In 1985, the name was changed to the Hector Ranger District, Finger Lakes National Forest.

Today, this National Forest is used for recreation, hunting, forestry, grazing of private livestock, preservation of wildlife habitat, education, and research. It is a treasure available for all of us to enjoy.

Bed & Breakfast: Red House Country Inn B&B, Picnic Area Road, (607) 546-8566

Distance between major roads:

Parmentor Road parking lot to E. Townline Road	1.6 miles
East Townline Road to Seneca Road	1.9 miles
Seneca Road to Potomac Road	1.0 mile
Potomac Road to Route 227	5.5 miles
Route 227 to Route 79	2.8 miles
Route 79 to Mark Smith Road	0.4 mile
Mark Smith Road to Mathews Road	1.8 miles
Mathews Road to Burnt Hill Road	0.6 mile
Burnt Hill Road to Picnic Area Road	1.6 miles
Picnic Area Road to Potomac Road	0.8 mile
Potomac Road to Seneca Road	4.0 miles
Seneca Road to County Road 146	0.1 mile
County Road 146 to Townsend Road	0.9 mile
Townsend Road to Ames Road	0.9 mile
Ames Road to Parmentor Road	1.0 mile
Parmentor Road to parking lot	0.3 mile

Trail Directions

- From the Interloken Trail parking lot, head east on Parmentor Road. In 0.6 mile, you pass Case Road/County Road 146. Continue straight, heading downhill for 1.0 mile on the dirt road, which changed its name to Butcher Hill Road.
- At East Townline Road turn right (S) onto this dirt road. It is paved in front of houses.

- Pass County Road 143, then turn right (W) onto Seneca Road.
- Follow Seneca Road for 1.0 mile passing Vesa Road and County Road 146/Case Road. At the stop sign, turn left (S) onto Potomac Road. This is a dirt road with rolling hills.
- After 1.0 mile, there is a stop sign and a Ballard Pasture sign as you approach paved Route 1. Continue straight (S).
- Pass a "Horse Crossing" sign. The terrain levels out. Two miles from Route 1 is a parking lot for the Backbone Trail and Foster Pond. Chicken Coop Road heads to the east. Continue straight.
- Pass the parking lot for Potomac Group Campground. The dirt road curves southwest and heads downhill.
- Continue south past Picnic Area Road and another parking area.
- Pass a National Forest sign, cross a small creek, and pass a few houses. Potomac Road ends at paved Route 227. You've come 9.4 miles so far.
- Turn right (SW) onto Route 227. Head downhill past a gravel pit and the Hector Town Hall. Continue on Route 227 for 2.8 miles.
- Turn right (W) onto paved Route 79. Travel 0.4 mile more and you are back to dirt roads.
- At Mark Smith Road, turn right (N). Pass some houses. Notice the waterfall to your left just before the "Leaving National Forest" sign.
- This is a steep uphill. Pass the Gorge Trail. The road winds back and forth and continues uphill.
- When the road-dead ends, turn left onto Mathews Road. Pass the Burnt Hill Trail, South Velie Pasture, and a parking area. A communications tower is to your right.
- Head downhill past a sign for Blueberry Patch and Interloken Trail and a parking area.
- At the stop sign, turn right onto Burnt Hill Road. Pass Ravine Trail. The road roller-coasters as it heads north. At the next stop sign, you've come 16.6 miles.
- Turn right onto Picnic Area Road. Head uphill past Backbone and Interloken Trails. The Red House Country Inn B&B is on your left. Straight ahead is Backbone Horse Camp.
- At the Blueberry Patch Campground, you may want to take a side trip to pick blueberries, if they're in season.
- Pass the Burnt Hill Trail parking area. Pass North Velie Pasture.
- Turn left and head north on Potomac Road. For 4.0 miles you're retracing a route you took earlier heading south. Pass Chicken Coop Road and Route 1.
- At the stop sign at Seneca Road turn right.

- Take the first left onto Case Road/County Road 146.
- In 0.9 mile, turn left onto Townsend Road/County Road 143. Only 2.2 more miles and you're done.
- Take the first right (N) onto Ames Road, which is a narrow dirt road. Pass Interloken Trail.
- Turn right and head east on Parmentor Road. The parking lot is on your right in 0.3 mile.

Date Bicycled: ______________

Notes:

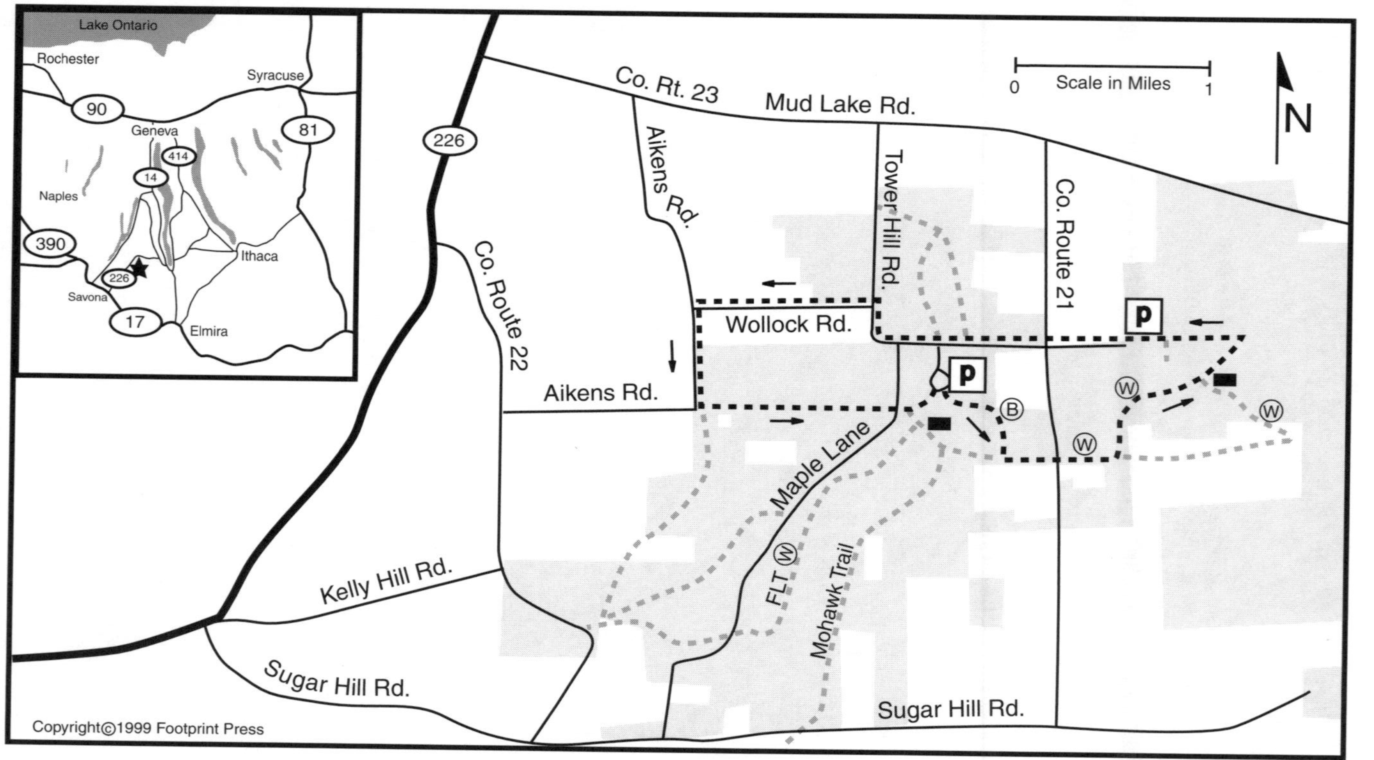

Sugar Hill State Forest

26.
Sugar Hill State Forest

Location: Southwest of Seneca Lake, Schuyler County
Directions: From Savona on Route 17, take Route 226 north. Turn east on County Route 23 (Mud Lake Road). Turn south on Tower Hill Road. This road will make a sharp left-hand turn and pass Maple Lane. The entrance to the tower parking area will be on the right.
Alternative Parking: At the east end of Tower Hill Road
Hiking Time: 3.5 hours
Biking Time: 1.5 hour
Length: 6.8 mile loop
Difficulty:
(mountain bike trail)
Surface: Dirt and gravel trails and roads
Trail Markings: White blazes, blue-and-orange plastic markers
Uses:
Dogs: OK on leash
Admission: Free
Contact: Finger Lakes Trail Conference
P.O. Box 18048
Rochester, NY 14618-0048
(716) 288-7191
http://www.fingerlakes.net/trailsystem

N.Y.S. Department of Environmental Conservation – Forestry
7291 Coon Road
Bath, NY 14810-9728
(607) 776-2165 ext. 10
http://www.dec.state.ny.us

The 9,085 acres of Sugar Hill State Forest is home to the Six Nations Horse and Snowmobile Trail network. The 40 miles of trails are used extensively by horses and their riders, particularly in the northern section.

The fire tower on top of Sugar Hill. Climb it for a magnificent view.

As a result, the majority of trails are mud wallows, ripped up by horse hoofs, and not pleasant for bicycling or walking. They also contain a conglomerate of trail marking methods. Trees and posts along the trail sport a wide array of blazes, markers, and signs. Each must mean something to somebody, but to a passing bicyclist they present a jumble of non-information.

The trail described here follows a mixture of driveable roads, wide logging roads, narrow gravel roads, and two track lanes that have held up well to the ravages of horse hooves. The definition of what constitutes a road is blurred in this area. Some portions of the trail described are on passable roads, others labeled as roads would require an all terrain vehicle, and others are blocked from cars altogether. You will be starting at the top of the hill. The first part of the trip will be an easy downhill, followed by climbing back up the hill. Then you'll descend and climb the other side of the hill, making this trip an aerobic workout.

The markings will be a combination of plastic markers and rectangular, white Finger Lakes Trail (FLT) blazes. You'll see round, orange snowmobile markers and round, blue horse trail markers. Sometimes signs give trail names, such as Onondaga Trail.

Sugar Hill derived its name from the abundant sugar maple trees, which once provided winter income for early settlers. Unfortunately, the shallow soils on this high land made farming unprofitable and early in the 19th century, forests began reclaiming the abandoned farmland. Conifers were planted in plantations which are still evident today as you ride the land.

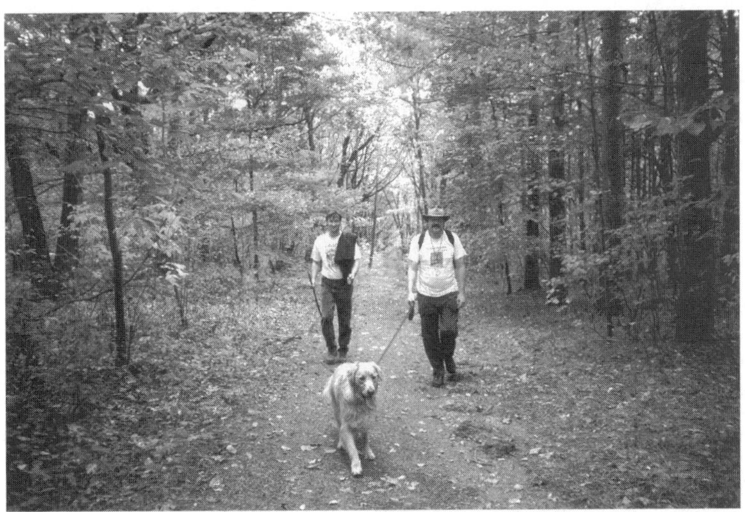

Stephen Keller, Jim Sherman, and Mr. Peabody enjoy the trails of Sugar Hill.

Your ride will begin and end near the fire tower which is the highest point in Schuyler County and the last remaining tower in the Finger Lakes area. You can climb it for a panoramic view of the hills separating Keuka and Seneca Lakes. Near the tower is a network of trails and straw bales that make up many archery courses.

In addition to the fire tower, the parking area has stalls for horses, picnic tables, water spigots, and outhouses. It's a popular camping area.

Camping: Allowed anywhere in Sugar Hill State Forest. Obtain a free camping permit from D.E.C. in Bath for stays of 3 nights or more, or groups of 10 or more individuals.

Trail Directions

- From the tower parking area, ride toward the horse stalls at the south corner of the camping area.
- Head left (E) on the trail that is blue blazed. This is the Onondaga Trail.
- At 0.5 mile, turn left (E). You are now on the white blazed Finger Lakes Trail, also called Seneca Trail.
- At 0.8 mile, cross Route 21.
- Turn left (N) at 1.0 mile.

- Cross a bridge.
- Cross a stream.
- At the "Y," follow the red-plastic-marked horse trail for an easier grade. This trail will rejoin the white-blazed Finger Lakes Trail shortly.
- Cross another stream.
- Pass the FLT lean-to at 1.9 mile.
- Pass a mowed grass trail to the left.
- Reach the barrier and parking area on Tower Hill Road at 2.7 miles.
- Ride uphill on Tower Hill Road, crossing Route 21 again.
- Pass the Cayuga Trail to the right and archery trails on both sides of the road.
- At 3.7 miles, pass the entrance to the tower parking area. Continue west.
- Pass Maple Lane on the left. (You can turn left here to shorten the ride.)
- Pass private Chipmunk Run on the left as Tower Hill Road bends sharply right.
- At 4.2 miles, turn left onto Wollock Road.
- When Wollock Road ends, turn left on Aikens Road.
- At 5.6 miles, Aikens Road will bend sharply right. Turn left onto a smaller lane and head uphill.
- Cross Maple Lane, passing a small parking area and rock barricades.
- At 6.7 miles, turn left onto a wide trail. Climb steeply uphill.
- Reach the horse stables, camping, and parking area.

Date Bicycled: ______________

Notes:

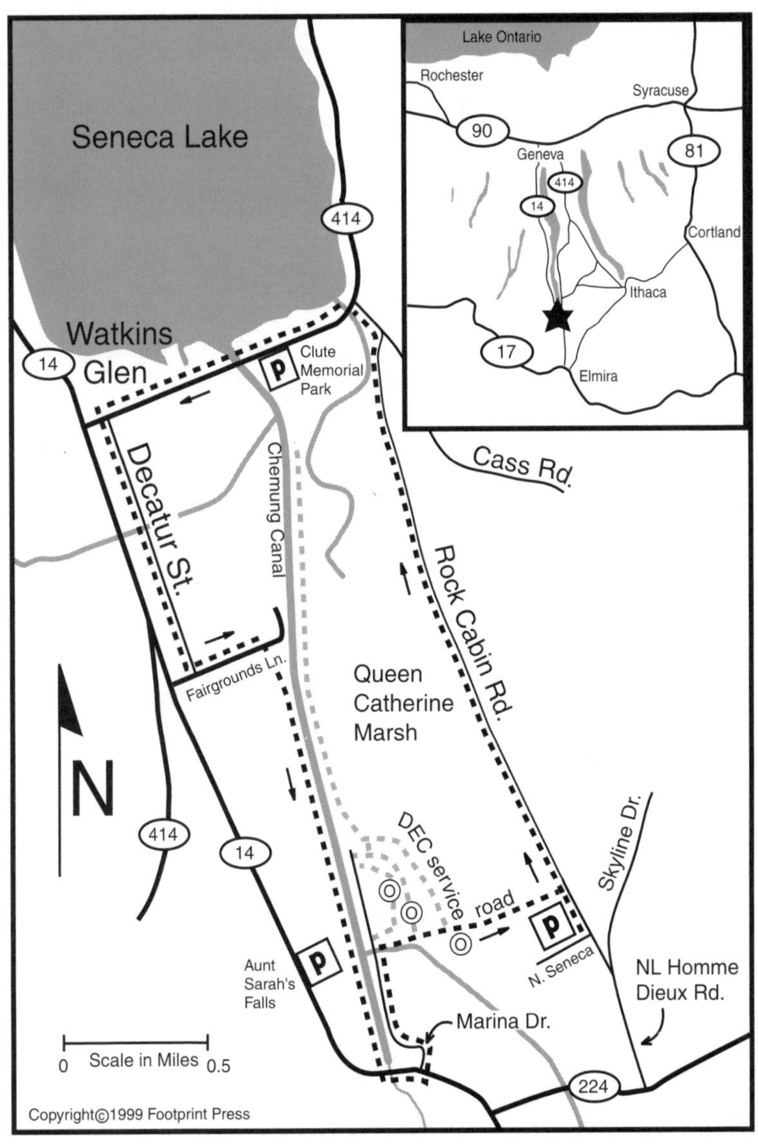

Queen Catherine Marsh

27.
Queen Catherine Marsh

Location: Between Watkins Glen and Montour Falls at the south end of Seneca Lake, Schuyler County
Directions: Take Route 14 south through Watkins Glen. Turn east on Route 224 and north on NL HommeDieux Road. Turn left on Rock Cabin Road and left on North Seneca Street. The grass D.E.C. parking area is near the corner of Rock Cabin Road, on North Seneca Street.
Alternative Parking: At the community center in Clute Memorial Park
Hiking Time: 1.0 hour
Length: 7.0 mile loop
Difficulty:
Surface: Dirt and grass trails and gravel roads
Trail Markings: Part of trail is orange blazed
Uses:
Dogs: OK
Admission: Free
Contact: N.Y.S. Department of Environmental Conservation – Wildlife
7291 Coon Road
Bath, NY 14810-9728
(607) 776-2165
http://www.dec.state.ny.us

Queen Catherine Marsh is an 882-acre protected wetland. Its man-made ditches and potholes attract shorebirds, waterfowl, muskrats, and turtles, among other wildlife. The wetlands act as a natural sponge for floodwaters, absorbing hundreds of thousands of gallons of floodwater per acre. Thirty species of butterflies breed in this area.

Once called Bad Indian Swamp, this cattail swamp at the south end of Seneca Lake was saved from the ravages of developers and swamp-pavers.

The shale cliffs along Rock Cabin Road.

Its current name is a tribute to a local native tribal monarch, Queen Catherine Montour, who died in 1804.

The Chemung Canal, which bisects Queen Catherine Marsh, once reached 23 miles south to Elmira. It was closed in 1887. The portion which remains today is part of the N.Y.S. Erie Canal System.

The 1.1-mile loop, Willow Walk, is a hiking-only trail within Queen Catherine Marsh. Its parking area is on Marina Drive. See *Take A Hike! Family Walks in the Finger Lakes and Genesee Valley Region* for details on this trail.

The bicycle route described here follows the unique Rock Cabin Road. This rarely used seasonal road is lined with shale cliffs on the east side and Queen Catherine Marsh far below on the west side. Watch carefully on the cliffs for Dutchman's breeches and squirrel corn. Dutchman's breeches' flowers resemble tiny off-white two-legged pantaloons dangling upside down from arched stems. Squirrel corn flowers look like the upside down bells of bleeding heart. The tubers of this plant resemble kernels of corn, thus the name.

The trail follows busy Route 414 for 1.0 mile but there are wide shoulders and a sidewalk to ride on away from cars. Then bicycle down two side streets before picking up an abandoned railroad bed.

Campgrounds: Havana Glen Park & Campground, Route 14 South, Montour Falls, (607) 535-9476

Municipal Campground & Marina, Marina Drive, Montour Falls

Warren W. Clute Memorial Park Camping Area, 521 East 4th Street, Watkins Glen, (607) 535-4438

Watkins Glen-Corning KOA, Route 414 South, Watkins Glen, (607) 535-7404

Six Nations Camping Area, Watkins Glen State Park, (800) 456-2267, http://www.park-net.com

Outfitters: Terrapin Outfitters, 123 3rd Street, Watkins Glen, (607) 535-5420

Watkins Sporting Goods, 123 4th Street, Watkins Glen, (607) 535-2756

Trail Description

- From the parking area, head east on North Seneca Road then turn left (N) on Rock Cabin Road.
- Pass the service road into Queen Catherine Marsh on the left.
- At 1.7 miles, the shale cliffs will begin on the right.
- Reach a "T" at 2.1 miles and turn left on Cass Road.
- Turn left at the stop sign onto Route 414.
- Cross Chemung Canal and then 3 railroad tracks.
- At the far end of Lafayette Park (with a square, white pavilion), turn left (SE) onto Decatur Street.
- Follow Decatur Street until it ends at a "T." You'll pass the high school, cross Glen Creek, and pass the Motor Racing Research and Public Libraries.
- At 4.1 miles, turn left on Fairgrounds Lane.
- Just before Ervay's Marina, turn right onto an abandoned railroad bed and pass a blue metal barrier.

- Walk your bike over an old bridge.
- At 5.6 miles, pass another blue metal barrier and turn left to follow the wide shoulder of Route 14 for 0.1 mile.
- Take the first left onto Marina Drive.
- Pass Erie Loop, Barge Road, then the other end of Erie Loop on your right as you ride along Marina Drive.
- At 6.3 miles, cross a bridge and turn immediately right onto the Scenic Trail. (Take the lower path, not the orange blazed stairs.)
- Continue straight passing a trail to the left.
- Cross a wooden bridge and reach a D.E.C. service road. Bear right on the service road. (The service road to the left is bikeable. It runs for 0.7 mile, paralleling Chemung Canal until it dead ends at the private Watkins Glen Yacht Club.)
- Pass a brown metal gate.
- Reach Rock Cabin Road and turn right.
- Turn right on North Seneca Street to return to the parking area.

Date Bicycled: _____________

Notes:

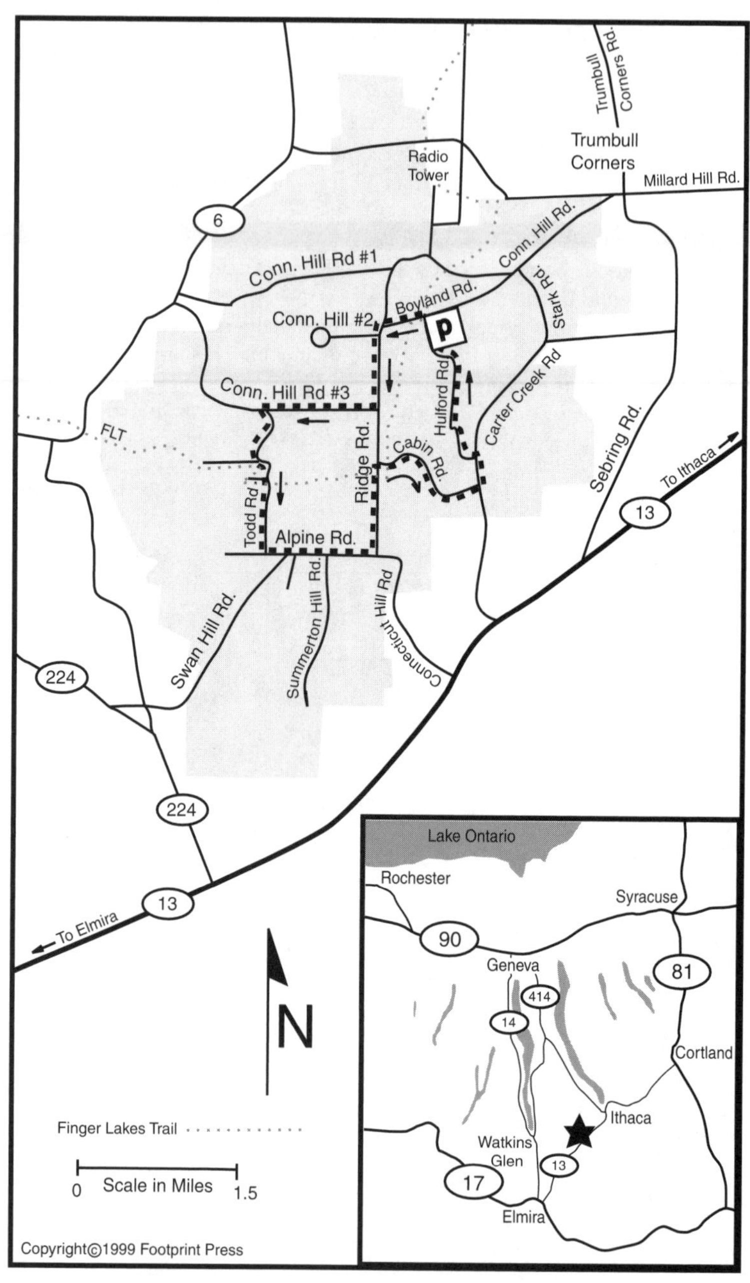

Connecticut Hill Wildlife Management Area

28.

Connecticut Hill Wildlife Management Area

Location: Midway between the south ends of Seneca Lake and Cayuga Lake, 13 miles southwest of Ithaca, Schuyler, and Tompkins Counties

Directions: From Ithaca, head south on Route 13. Turn west on Millard Hill Road, 1 mile beyond the junction with Routes 34/96. Pass through Trumbull Corners, then turn left on Connecticut Hill Road. Continue straight onto Boyland Road. Park along the road, near the corner of Boyland Road and Hulford Road.

Alternative Parking: Anywhere along the roads within the area

Biking Time: 2 hours

Length: 9.1 mile loop

Difficulty:

Surface: Seasonal gravel roads

Trail Markings: None

Uses:   

Dogs: OK

Admission: Free

Contact: N.Y.S. Department of Environmental Conservation
1285 Fisher Avenue
Cortland, NY 13045
(607) 753-3095
http://www.dec.state.ny.us

Connecticut Hill is the largest wildlife management area in New York State, covering 11,654 acres. It is part of the Appalachian Highlands, which is distinctive as a belt of high, rough land. Because of this, the area is rugged bicycling. The trail described follows seasonal gravel roadbeds but the terrain is always hilly, sometimes with steep sections as it winds on and off the plateau. Expect an aerobic workout.

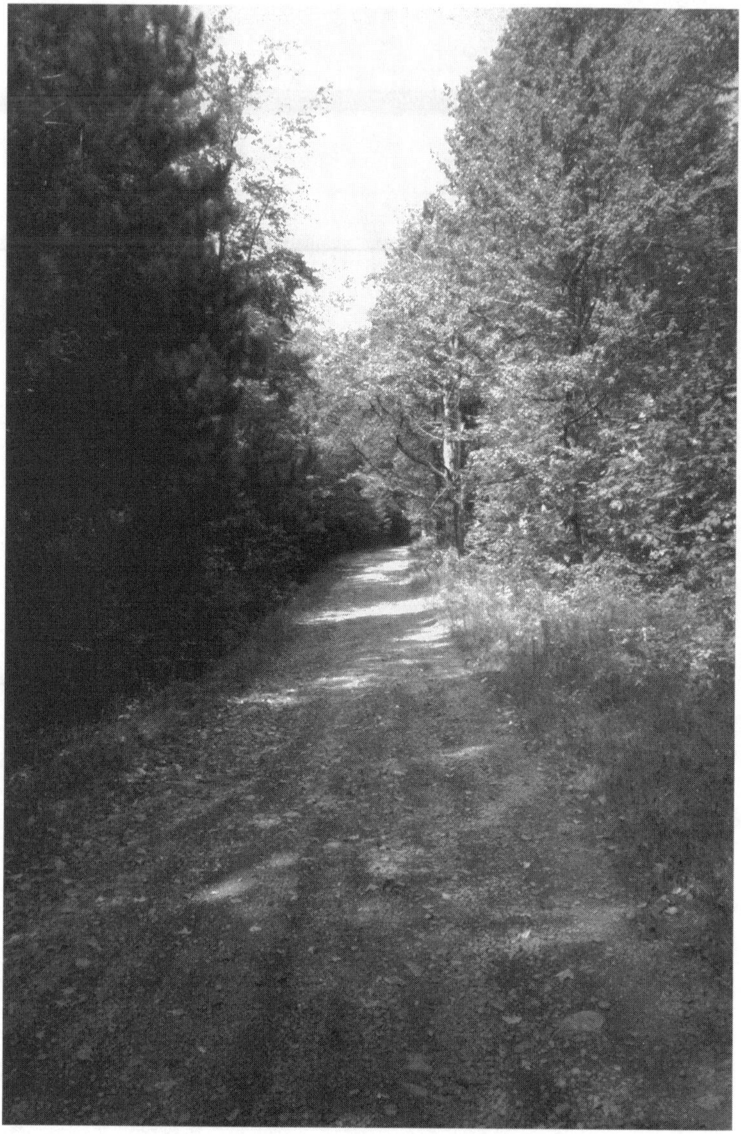

The roads (bike trails) in Connecticut Hill.

Besides the steep hills, the other challenge of this area is that most roads are not labeled. You need to be able to follow the map and directions to traverse this area successfully. Then too, you'll find that many of the roads are called Connecticut Hill Road, sometimes with a number and sometimes without.

Indians were the first inhabitants to roam this area. They were driven out by George Washington's troops in the late 1700s. From 1800 until 1850, the land was owned by the state of Connecticut and then sold to private landowners. However, the name, Connecticut Hill, stuck.

By the mid-19th century, much of the land in this area had been cleared for cultivation and pasture. But the farms languished due to poor soil conditions, and many farms were abandoned. By 1926, only 20 of the original 109 farms remained in operation. Through the Federal Resettlement Administration, the government began buying farmland and the game refuge came into existence.

Trail Directions

- From the intersection of Boyland Road and Hulford Road, head west on Boyland Road.
- Reach a "T," and turn left (S) onto Ridge Road (also called Connecticut Hill Road).
- Pass Connecticut Hill Road #2 on the right. At 1.2 miles, turn right (W) on Connecticut Hill Road #3.
- Take the first left (S) onto Todd Road and head downhill.
- Turn left to continue south steeply downhill on Todd Road.
- Cross a new bridge at 3.1 miles.
- Pass a road on the right, then the crossing of the white-blazed Finger Lakes Trail. Continue gradually downhill.
- Reach a "T," and turn left (E) onto Alpine Road.
- Pass two roads on the right that are close together.
- Pass Summerton Hill Road on the right as you traverse steep hills.
- At 4.9 miles, reach the junction with Ridge Road (Connecticut Hill Road) and turn left (NE), heading uphill.
- The white-blazed Finger Lakes Trail will cross the road.
- At Cabin Road, turn right (E). Ride a steep downhill then emerge to open fields.
- At 7.2 miles, turn left (NW) on Carter Creek Road.
- Cross Carter Creek.

- 0.2 mile after crossing Carter Creek, turn left (W) on Hulford Road. Head uphill for a while and then the road will level out.
- Reach Boyland Road where you will find your car.

Date Bicycled: ______________

Notes:

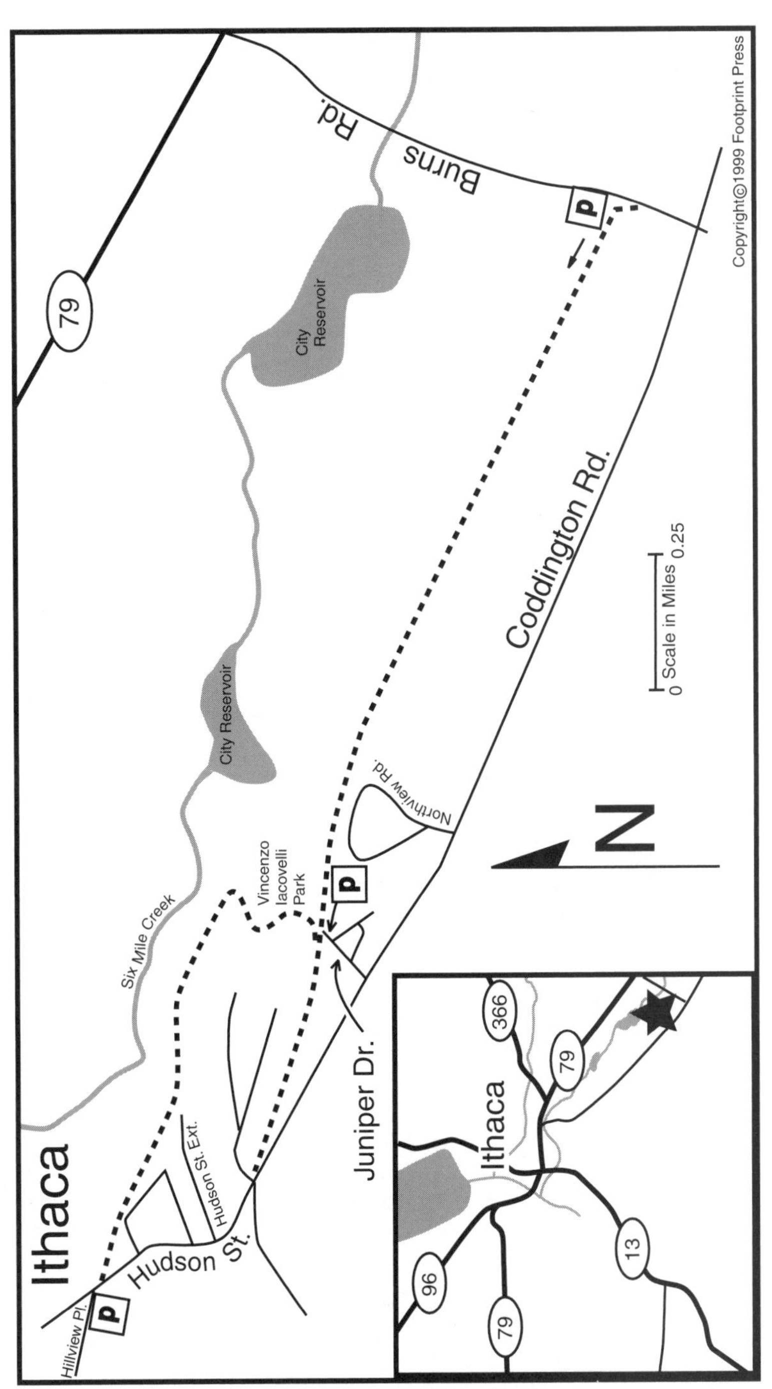

South Hill Recreation Way

29.
South Hill Recreation Way

Location: Ithaca, Tompkins County

Directions: From Ithaca follow Route 79 east. Turn right (S) on Burns Road. Parking is on the west side of Burns Road at a sign for "South Hill Recreation Way Parking." Watch for the green-and-white, square bicycle signs.

Alternative Parking: A small parking area on Hillview Place across from the trail end-point on Hudson Street
At the end of Juniper Drive

Biking Time: 1.5 hour

Length: 7.0 miles round trip

Difficulty:

Surface: Packed gravel trail and a short paved section

Trail Markings: Yellow-and-brown wooden signs "South Hill Recreation Way" and mile marker signs every half mile

Uses:

Dogs: OK on leash

Admission: Free

Contact: Town of Ithaca Highway/Parks Department
106 Seven Mile Drive
Ithaca, NY 14850
(607) 273-8035

This trail was developed in 1986 as a N.Y.S. Environmental Quality Bond Act Project. Today, it's a gem for all of us to enjoy. It follows the abandoned rail bed of the Cayuga and Susquehanna, which was built in 1849 to haul coal from the Pennsylvania mines to a canal in Ithaca. Eventually it merged with the Delaware, Lackawanna, and Western Railroad and was abandoned in 1957.

The terrain is gradual hills, mostly downhill on the outbound leg and uphill for the return. You're riding in the Six Mile Creek Gorge. This creek is currently dammed for use as a water supply for Ithaca. Hiking paths lead off the biking trail into the gorge. Numbered posts are positioned along part of the route at the western end. Brochures that explain the plant communities you'll pass are available along the trail. Here's a synopsis.

1. **Weedy Invasives** – European honeysuckle in bush form grows here.
2. **Tree of Heaven** – This tree was imported from China as a hardy tree that can withstand harsh urban conditions.
3. **Shagbark Hickory** – A native tree with shaggy, pealing gray bark.
4. **Goldenrod** – Its bright yellow flowers are a sign of fall.
5. **Black Locust** – A tree with sweet-smelling flowers in spring and compound elliptical leaflets.
6. **Cottonwood** – Also known as poplar or quaking aspen, this is a fast growing tree.
7. **Black Walnut** – A tree prized for its wood.
8. **Fossils** – Look for the marine animals that once inhabited the shallow sea that covered this area.
9. **Simple and Vascular Plants** – Moss and wild geraniums grow on the rocks behind you.
10. **Old Growth Forest** – These trees are 75 to 100 years old or older.
11. **Non-Native Species of a Different Sort** – The unusual stones here are glacial erratics that were brought south by the glaciers.
12. **Old Farm Fields** – 50 years ago, this area of small trees was a farm field.

Bed & Breakfasts:	Hanshaw House, 15 Sapsucker Woods Road, Ithaca, (607) 257-1437
	Hound & Hare, 1031 Hanshaw Road, Ithaca, (607) 257-2821
	Sweet Dreams B&B, 228 Wood Street, Ithaca (607) 272-7727
Bike Shops:	The Bike Rack, 414 College Avenue, Ithaca, (607) 272-1010
	Cayuga Mountain Bike Shop, 138 West State Street, Ithaca, (607) 277-6821
Boat Tour:	Cayuga Lake Cruises, 704 W. Buffalo Street, Ithaca (800) 951-5901
Campgrounds:	Buttermilk Falls State Park, Route 13, Ithaca, (607) 273-5761
	Robert H. Treman State Park, Route 327, Ithaca, (607) 273-3440
	Spruce Row, 2271 Kraft Road, Ithaca, (607) 387-9225
Outfitter:	The Outdoor Store, 206 East State Street, Ithaca, (607) 273-3891

The sign at the western end of South Hill Recreation Way.

Trail Directions

- From the Burns Road trail entrance, head downhill.
- At 1.4 miles, pass a barricade.
- At 1.7 miles, pass Juniper Drive. Parking is available here.
- Pass a trail to the right, to Vincenzo Iacovelli Park.
- Reach Coddinton Road at 2.3 miles. Turn around and retrace your path.
- At the first junction, turn left into Vincenzo Iacovelli Park. The trail will be paved for a short while.
- Watch for the numbered posts that describe the plant communities in the Six Mile Creek Gorge.
- Reach Hudson Street at 4.0 miles. Turn around and retrace your path.
- Turn left at the "T."
- Pass Juniper Drive.
- Pass the barricade at 5.6 miles.
- Reach Burns Road.

Date Bicycled: _______________

Notes:

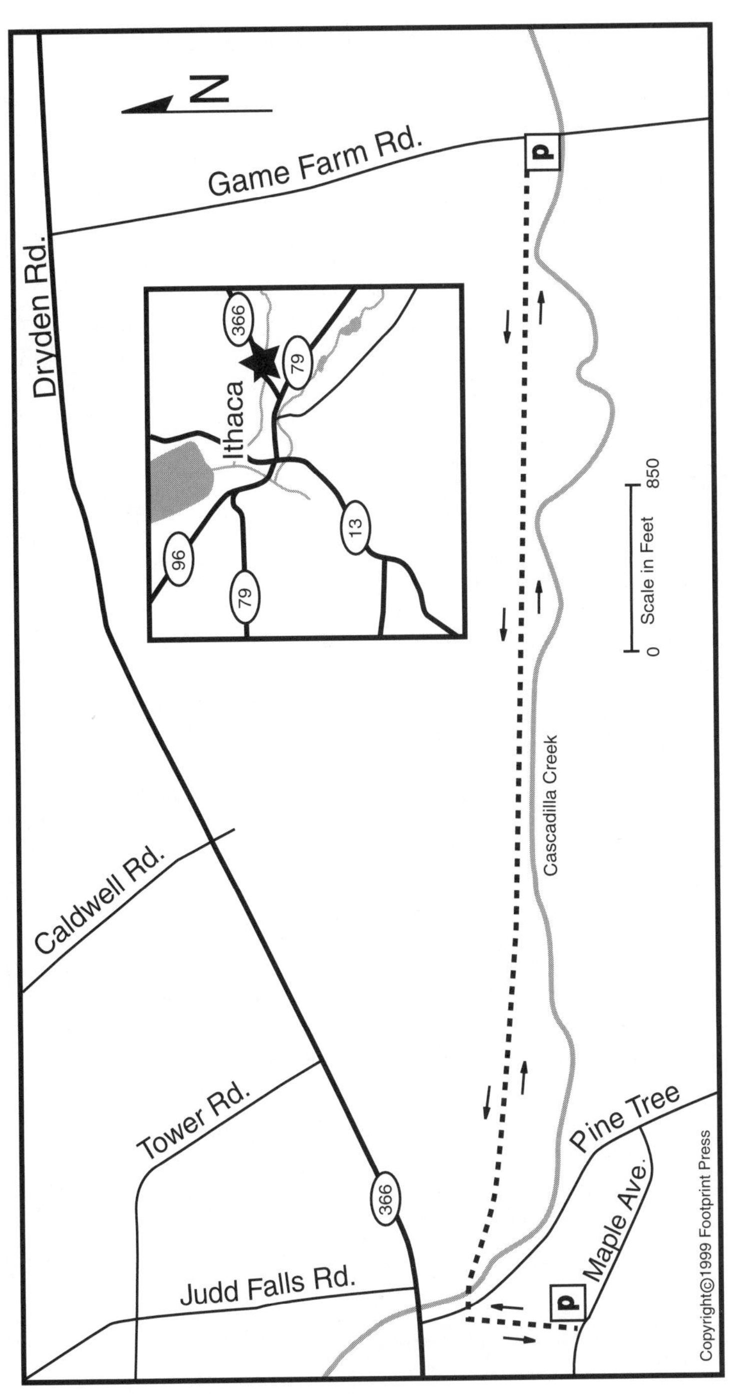

East Ithaca Recreation Way

30.
East Ithaca Recreation Way

Location: Ithaca, Tompkins County
Directions: From Ithaca follow Route 366 east. Turn south on Game Farm Road. The parking area is on the west side of Game Farm Road, 0.6 mile from Route 366. Watch for the green-and-white, square bicycle signs.
Alternative Parking: Along the road at Maple Avenue.
Biking Time: 20 minutes
Length: 2.2 miles round trip
Difficulty:
Surface: Paved trail
Trail Markings: Wooden mile marker signs every quarter mile
Uses:
Dogs: OK on leash
Admission: Free
Contact: Cornell Plantations
One Plantation Road
Ithaca, NY 14850-2799
(607) 255-3020

Here's an easy trail for beginners or families with young children. It's a short trail with scenic views of a creek along the way. To avoid the short steep section, turn around at the Cascadilla Creek bridge.

Bed & Breakfasts: Hanshaw House, 15 Sapsucker Woods Road, Ithaca, (607) 257-1437

Hound & Hare, 1031 Hanshaw Road, Ithaca, (607) 257-2821

Sweet Dreams B&B, 228 Wood Street, Ithaca (607) 272-7727

Bike Shops: The Bike Rack, 414 College Avenue, Ithaca, (607) 272-1010

	Cayuga Mountain Bike Shop, 138 West State Street, Ithaca, (607) 277-6821
Boat Tour:	Cayuga Lake Cruises, 704 West Buffalo Street, Ithaca, (800) 951-5901
Campgrounds:	Buttermilk Falls State Park, Route 13, Ithaca, (607) 273-5761
	Robert H. Treman State Park, Route 327, Ithaca, (607) 273-3440
	Spruce Row, 2271 Kraft Road, Ithaca, (607) 387-9225
Outfitter:	The Outdoor Store, 206 East State Street, Ithaca, (607) 273-3891

Trail Directions

- From the parking area on Game Farm Road, head west on the paved trail.
- Cascadilla Creek will be to your left.
- At 1.0 mile, cross Cascadilla Creek and Pine Tree Road on bridges.
- The paved trail bends sharply left and heads uphill.
- At 1.1 miles, reach Maple Avenue.
- Turn around and retrace your path back to Game Farm Road.

Date Bicycled: ______________

Notes:

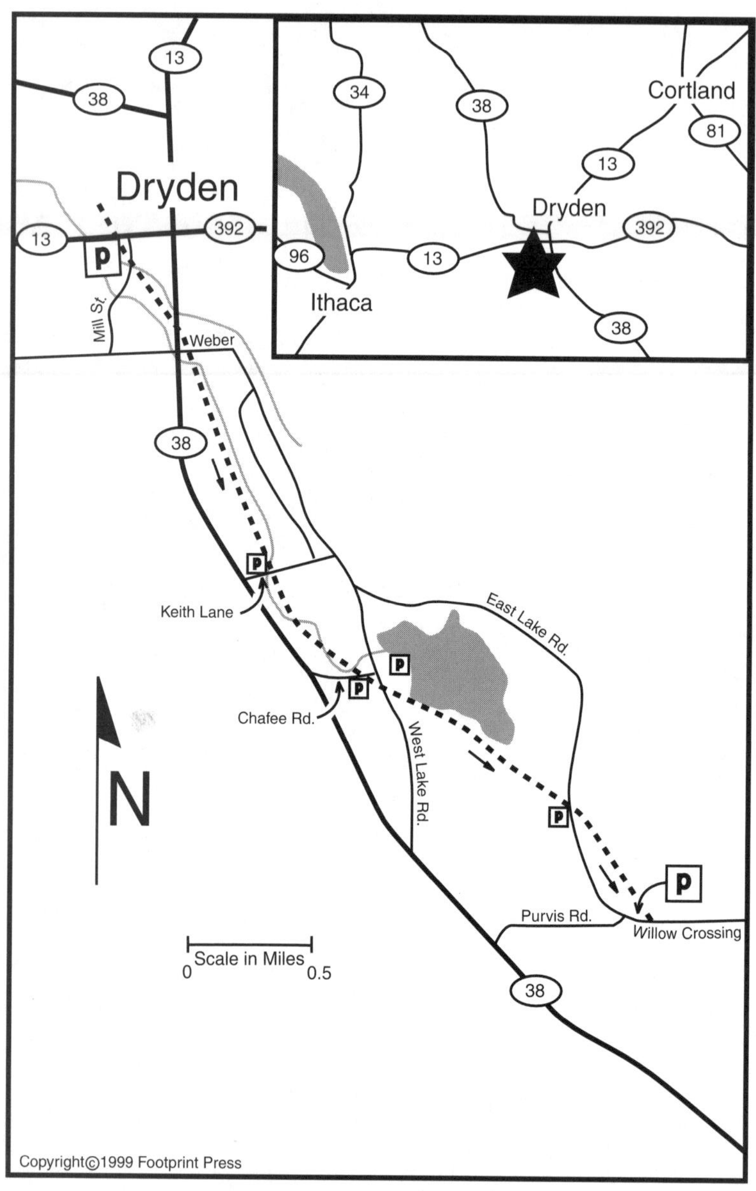

Dryden Lake Park Trail

31.
Dryden Lake Park Trail

Location: Dryden, east of Ithaca, Tompkins and Cortland Counties

Directions: From Ithaca follow Route 13, east to Dryden. Park at or near the Dryden Agway with permission (59 West Main Street, across from Rochester Street).

Alternative Parking: Keith Lane
Chafee Road
Dryden Lake Park
Lake Road
A parking area on Willow Crossing

Biking Time: 1.25 hours

Length: 8.4 miles round trip

Difficulty:

Surface: Mowed grass and packed gravel trail

Trail Markings: Square blue-and-white metal signs "Dryden Lake Park Trail," and mile markers every half mile along the trail

Uses:   

Dogs: OK on leash

Admission: Free

Contact: Town of Dryden
65 East Main Street
Dryden, NY 13053
(607) 844-8619
http://www.dryden.ny.us

The Southern Central Railroad was built in 1865 to connect Sayre, Pennsylvania to Auburn. It became part of the Lehigh Valley System and was abandoned in 1976. The tracks were taken up and sold for scrap in 1979.

The beginning of the trail in Dryden was once the location of a private feed mill. Later, local farmers established a cooperative called the "Farmers

Escape to a quiet country trail in Dryden.

Feed and Milling Corporation." GLF (which became Agway) modernized the grain mill in the 1930s.

Dryden Lake Park is 0.1 mile north of the West Lake Road crossing. This park offers fishing access, picnic tables and a pavilion, rest rooms, a playground, and an observation deck over the lake. The area was once an Indian campground and home of an early sawmill and railroad ice station.

Interpretive signs along this easy-riding trail offer information on the animals and plants that inhabit the area. Birds are abundant, and beaver activity is evident if you watch carefully.

Bed & Breakfasts: The Candlelight Inn, 49 West Main Street, Dryden, (607) 844-4321

Serendipity B&B, 15 North Street, Dryden, (607) 844-9589

Thorn House, 1899 Gee Hill Road, Dryden, (607) 844-9562

Ice Cream: Purple Lion, 52 North Street, Dryden, (607) 844-9636

Trail Directions

- From Agway, head southeast on the trail.
- Cross a railroad bridge.
- Cross Mill Street.
- At 0.6 mile, cross Route 38 then quickly cross Weber Street.
- Pass a 1-mile marker and bench. A swamp is on the right.
- Cross Keith Lane. (Parking is available here.)
- Pass a 2-mile marker and bench.
- Cross Chafee Road. (Parking is available here.)
- Cross West Lake Road. Dryden Lake Park (with parking) is a short distance to the left.
- Pass a deck overlooking Dryden Lake.
- Pass a 3-mile marker and bench.
- Cross East Lake Road. (Parking is available here.)
- Pass a 4-mile marker and bench.
- The trail ends at a parking area on Willow Crossing. Turn around and retrace your path.

Date Bicycled: ______________

Notes:

Rides in Cayuga & Onondaga Counties

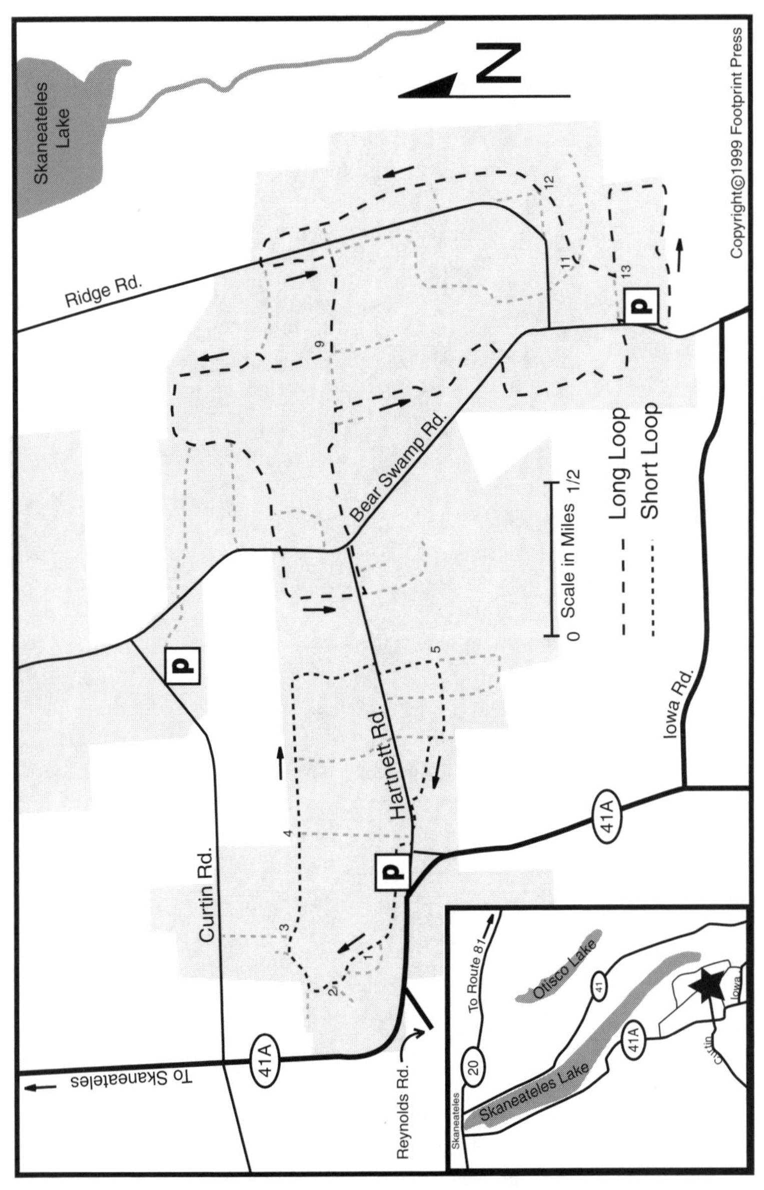

Bear Swamp State Forest
Short Loop and Long Loop

32.
Bear Swamp State Forest – Short Loop

Location: At the southwest end of Skaneateles Lake, Cayuga County

Directions: From Skaneateles, head south on Route 41A. Pass Curtin Road and Reynolds Road. Turn left on the next unmarked dirt road. A brown and yellow D.E.C. sign is on the right side of Route 41A, "Bear Swamp State Forest." Park along the dirt road where you see a wooden kiosk at the trailhead on the left side of the road.

Alternative Parking: Anywhere along the dirt road (Hartnett Road)

Hiking Time: 2 hours

Biking Time: 1 hour

Length: 3.4 mile loop

Difficulty: (mountain bike trail)

Surface: Dirt trails

Trail Markings: Two-inch round yellow disks with black lettering, "N.Y.S. Environmental Conservation Ski Trail." Also, many intersections have six-inch brown signs with yellow numbers posted on trees above head level.

Uses:  

Dogs: OK

Admission: Free

Contact: N.Y.S. Department of Environmental Conservation
P.O. Box 5170, Fisher Road
Cortland, NY 13045-5170
(607) 753-3095
http://www.dec.state.ny.us

This 3,316-acre state forest is traversed with 13 miles of trails through shady forest. Over 10,000 years ago, the glaciers sculpted the Finger Lakes, leaving steep valley walls and flat-topped ridges. Native Americans used this

area as hunting grounds. After the Revolutionary War, veterans and their families cleared the forests and settled the area. Farming continued through the Civil War and slowly declined as the soil was depleted, until the Great Depression of 1929 hastened farm abandonment. As with the other State Forest land, this land was purchased in the 1930s and was replanted by the Civilian Conservation Corps with red pine, Norway spruce, and larch. You'll be passing through these replanted forests, now a mix of conifers and hardwoods.

Bear Swamp State Forest is managed using the multiple-use concept. This concept includes maintaining wildlife habitat, harvesting wood products, and encouraging recreational uses. The roads in Bear Swamp State Forest are rough but navigable by a vehicle. They are seasonal use roads that are not plowed in the winter.

The trails are well marked with round, yellow ski trail markers. When in doubt, follow the marked trail. It can be muddy after rain and has the challenge of roots to traverse. Hills tend to be long, but not particularly steep.

Trail Directions (short, dark dashed lines on page 141 map)

- Head north on the trail past the wooden kiosk.
- Cross a wooden bridge.
- Cross a corduroy bridge.
- Cross two more wooden bridges.
- After 0.4 mile, reach intersection #1. (Numbered signs are on trees above head level.)
- Turn right to stay on the marked trail, which is an old logging road. Notice the stumps and cut treetops where wood was harvested for firewood and pulpwood.
- At 0.6 mile, reach a junction and turn right to stay on the marked trail.
- Shortly, reach intersection #2 and bear right on the marked trail, an old fire road. This road is a relic of the 1930s, when the young conifer plantation needed fire lanes for access and protection.
- Reach a "T" intersection at 0.8 mile and turn right.
- Around 1 mile, watch carefully. Follow the markers going right, leaving the well-trodden trail.
- Reach intersection #3 and turn right (S) on the wider trail. Notice the thinned, hardwood forest to the west vs. the crowded, unmanaged red pine forest to the east.
- Shortly the trail bends left (E) and heads downhill.

- At 1.5 miles, a trail will head off to the right, continue straight (SE), downhill.
- Reach intersection #4 at 1.6 miles and continue straight, downhill. (A right here is the shortcut back to Hartnett Road.)
- Continue straight past a trail off to the right.
- Cross several bog areas with makeshift bridges.
- At 2.4 miles, cross a flowing spring. Head uphill.
- Reach Hartnett Road (a small gravel road) and turn right, uphill. Immediately, look for a trail to the left and follow it uphill through a young hardwood forest of native maple, ash, and cherry trees.
- Reach intersection #5 at 2.8 miles and turn right, uphill.
- Cross a gravel road and continue straight, uphill.
- At 3.0 miles, reach a "T" and turn right (N).
- Shortly, the marked trail veers left. (Straight goes to a road.)
- At 3.2 miles, reach Hartnett Road but turn left and continue on the trail, parallel to the road.
- Emerge to the road and bear left on Hartnett Road.
- Pass a trail to the right then arrive at the parking area.

Date Bicycled: ____________

Notes:

33.
Bear Swamp State Forest – Long Loop

Location: At the southwest end of Skaneateles Lake, Cayuga County

Directions: From Route 41A head south past Curtin Road, Reynolds Road, and the Colonial Lodge. Turn left on Iowa Road. Take the first left on Bear Swamp Road. The parking area will be on the right up 0.2 mile.

Alternative Parking: At any road/trail intersection, or the parking area on Curtin Road.

Hiking Time: 4 hours

Biking Time: 1.5 hours

Length: 7.8 mile loop

Difficulty: (mountain bike trail)

Surface: Dirt trails

Trail Markings: Two-inch round yellow disks with black lettering, "N.Y.S. Environmental Conservation Ski Trail." Also, many intersections have six-inch brown signs with yellow numbers posted on trees above head level.

Uses: 

Dogs: OK

Admission: Free

Contact: N.Y.S. Department of Environmental Conservation
P.O. Box 5170, Fisher Road
Cortland, NY 13045-5170
(607) 753-3095
http://www.dec.state.ny.us

Trail Directions (long, dark dashed lines on page 141 map)

- From the south parking lot on Bear Swamp Road, head southwest past a yellow sign, "motorized vehicles prohibited." Bear Swamp Road will be on your right.
- The trail bends left and heads uphill.

- Cross a small wooden bridge and continue uphill.
- Pass through a forest of red pine and Norway spruce planted in 1932–1933. Notice the old stone walls to your right (NE) in the dense woods.
- The trail, an old fire lane, bends left (N) and heads gradually downhill.
- The trail bends left (W) and heads uphill.
- Crest the hill and head down. Notice the large fern field to the right.
- At the next junction (#13), turn right (N), uphill. (Left returns to the parking area.) At this point, you've completed 1 mile.
- Reach intersection #11 and continue straight (NE). Follow the markers, uphill to a crest and then down.
- The trail bends left and heads uphill again.
- At 1.4 miles, reach intersection #12. Turn right (E) and follow the markers downhill.
- The trail bends left, dips, then begins a long, slow climb.
- Continue straight, past a trail to the left, for a long, slow downhill.
- Continue uphill past a trail to the left. The trail narrows and begins to roll.
- At 2.4 miles, cross a bridge. When the leaves are off the trees, there's a view of Skaneateles Lake from this area.
- At 2.5 miles, turn left, following the markers. The trail continues straight here so watch carefully.
- After a steep uphill, cross Ridge Road. Bear left on the marked trail across the road and head parallel to Ridge Road heading south.
- Head through a pine woods.
- At 2.9 miles, reach a "T" and turn right (W) on a wide dirt trail.
- After a speed bump, reach intersection #9. Turn right and cross another speed bump.
- At 3.5 miles, pass an old stone foundation. Notice the myrtle and old apple trees; remnants of an old farm house.
- Reach a "T" and turn left. This section is not as hilly but can be dotted with huge mud puddles during wet times of the year.
- At 4.1 miles, reach a trail junction and bear left. (Right goes to Curtin Road and a parking area.)
- Stay on the wide dirt trail as a trail heads off on the right.
- A long downhill will turn into a grass path.
- Cross Bear Swamp Road at 4.9 miles, then another long downhill.
- Cross a wooden bridge.
- At 5.3 miles, cross Hartnett Road. Immediately across the road turn left (E) and parallel Hartnett Road.

  [**Side Trip:** The trail straight ahead is a 4-minute walk or 1-minute ride to a picturesque overlook of the Bear Mountain Swamp with its balsam fir, swamp-meadow grass, and alder patches.]

- The trail will be level, followed by a short, steep downhill.
- Cross a small dirt road and continue straight.
- Cross a wooden bridge before crossing Bear Swamp Road at 5.5 miles.
- You're heading northeast up a long hill.
- Continue straight past the next trail intersection on the right.
- Cross a streambed.
- Traverse rolling terrain on a narrow woods path.
- Several logging trails intersect. Stay on the marked trail.
- At 6.5 miles, turn left (S) on a wide trail.
- At 6.8 miles, stay on the marked trail as it turns right, off the wide trail.
- At 6.9 miles, cross Bear Swamp Road and continue straight, downhill through fields of jewelweed on the forest floor.
- At 7.7 miles, cross Bear Swamp Road again. Take an immediate right (S) on the trail parallel to Bear Swamp Road, heading south, back to the parking area.

Date Bicycled: _______________

Notes:

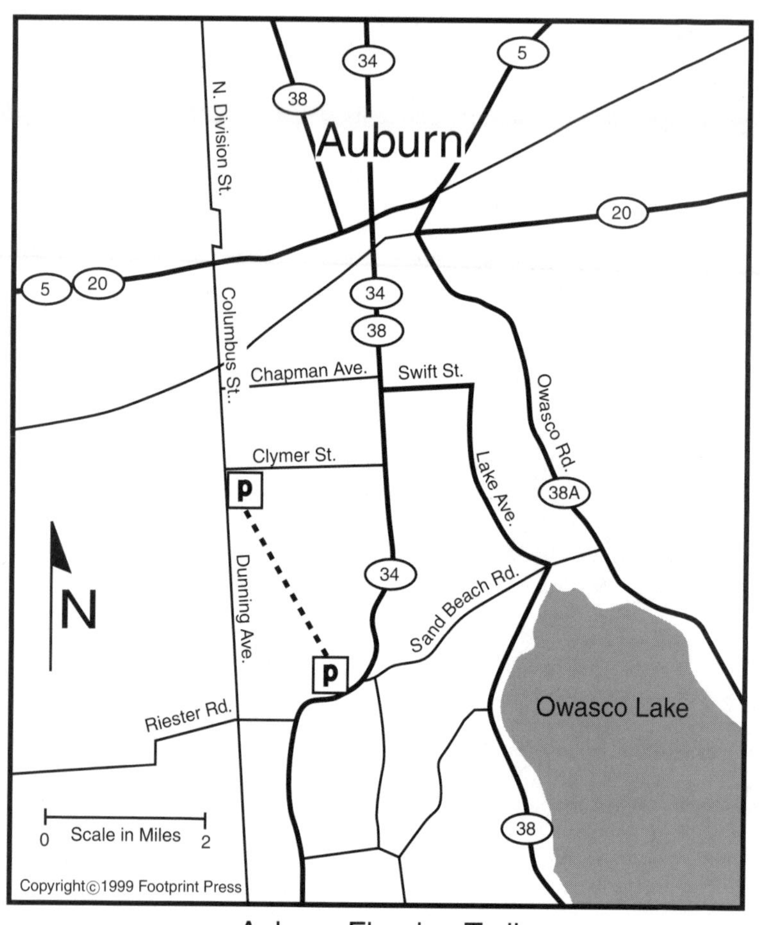

Auburn-Fleming Trail

34.
Auburn – Fleming Trail

Location: South of Auburn, Cayuga County
Directions: From Route 5 & 20, turn south on Columbus Street. Parking is on the east side of Dunning Avenue, south of Clymer Street. It is marked by a brown sign with yellow lettering "Cayuga County Trail, Auburn – Fleming"
Alternative Parking: Route 34, southwest of Sand Beach Road
Hiking Time: 60 minutes
Biking Time: 30 minutes
Length: 2 miles round trip
Difficulty:
Surface: Dirt and cinder trail
Trail Markings: None
Uses:

Dogs: OK
Admission: Free
Contact: County Planner
Cayuga County Planning Board
160 Genesee Street
Auburn, NY 13021-1276
(315) 253-1276

Michele Beilman
Cayuga County Parks and Trails Commission
East Lake Road
Auburn, N.Y. 13021
(315) 253-5611

The Auburn – Fleming Trail uses an abandoned railroad bed. There's not much elevation change but the terrain roller coasters and is populated with enough deteriorating railroad ties to make the ride interesting. It's a pleasant walk or ride in a four-foot-wide tunnel through trees.

Bed and Breakfasts: Springside Inn, Route 38 South, Auburn, (315) 252-724

Irish Rose, Auburn, (315) 255-0196

Angel's Rest B&B, Auburn, (315) 255-9188

Trail Directions

- The trail begins behind (W) the sign, with a rough ride over old wooden ties buried in the ground.
- After 0.25 mile, cross a stream on a metal grate bridge.
- A marsh will be on the left. Cross its outlet over a wooden railroad tie bridge.
- The ride now gets smoother.
- Cross a second railroad tie bridge.
- Unmarked trails lead off to the left. (Please stay on the Auburn – Fleming Trail. The trails to the left are on private property.) Continue straight.
- There's a dip in the trail and then a farm lane crossing.
- Cross another railroad tie bridge over a creek. The trail begins to roll up and down like a roller coaster.
- A trail to the right heads to a farm.
- Pass some small side loops carved by mountain bikers.
- The trail ends at Route 34. Turn around and retrace your path.

Date Bicycled: ______________

Notes:

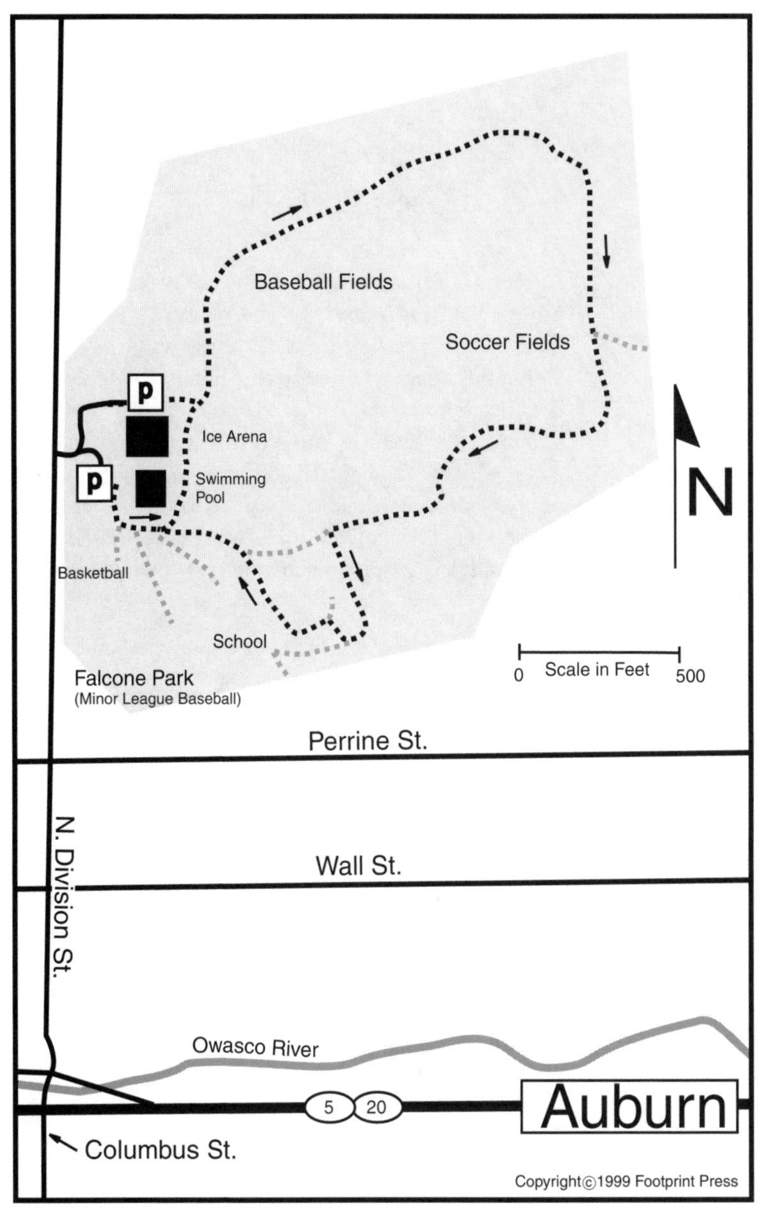
Baseball Fields
Soccer Fields
P
Ice Arena
P
Swimming
Pool
Basketball
School
Falcone Park
(Minor League Baseball)
N
0 Scale in Feet 500
Perrine St.
Wall St.
N. Division St.
Owasco River
5
20
Auburn
Columbus St.
Copyright©1999 Footprint Press

Casey Park

35.
Casey Park

Location: Auburn (north of Routes 5 & 20 on North Division Street), Cayuga County

Directions: From Route 5 & 20, turn north at the traffic light on Columbus Street. (The large blue building of Auburn Technology is on this corner.) Continue north as Columbus Street turns into North Division Street. The parking lot for Casey Park is off North Division Street, next to Falcon Baseball Park, and across the street from Technology Park (an industrial park). Bear right as you enter and park past the swimming pool.

Alternative Parking: None

Hiking Time: 30 minutes

Biking Time: 10 minutes

Length: 1 mile loop

Difficulty:

Surface: Paved

Trail Markings: None

Uses:

Dogs: OK on leash

Admission: Free

Contact: Casey Park
North Division Street
Auburn, NY 13021
(315) 253-4247

Casey Park is a 44-acre sports complex. It includes an Olympic-sized, outdoor swimming pool, an ice skating rink, soccer and softball fields, basketball courts, horseshoe pits, tennis courts, bocce courts, and picnic areas. A paved path (nicely resurfaced in 1998) winds through the park.

As you head north off Routes 5 and 20 on North Division Street, you'll cross railroad tracks. Pull off at the overlook as the road crosses the Owasco River to see a pretty waterfall.

Bed and Breakfasts: Springside Inn, Route 38 South, Auburn, (315) 252-7247

Irish Rose, Auburn, (315) 255-0196

Angel's Rest B&B, Auburn, (315) 255-9188

Trail Directions

- Follow the paved path from the south end of the parking lot.
- Bear left past three trails to the right. (The first goes to a basketball court, the second to a school, and the third to a pavilion.)
- Pass a pavilion on the right and several trails on the left, which lead to the pool and ice rink.
- Pass a trail to the right, which leads to the baseball field.
- Pass a trail on the left, which leads uphill to a parking lot.
- The trail will bend right and pass a shed and baseball fields.
- A trail to the left (opposite soccer fields) heads through the woods to Washington Street.
- At the next intersection, turn left and head uphill. (Continue straight if you want to avoid the hill.)
- Turn right at the next junction and then bear left (right goes to the amphitheater) and pass a pavilion as you head downhill.
- At the "T," turn left to return to the parking lot.

Date Bicycled: ______________

Notes:

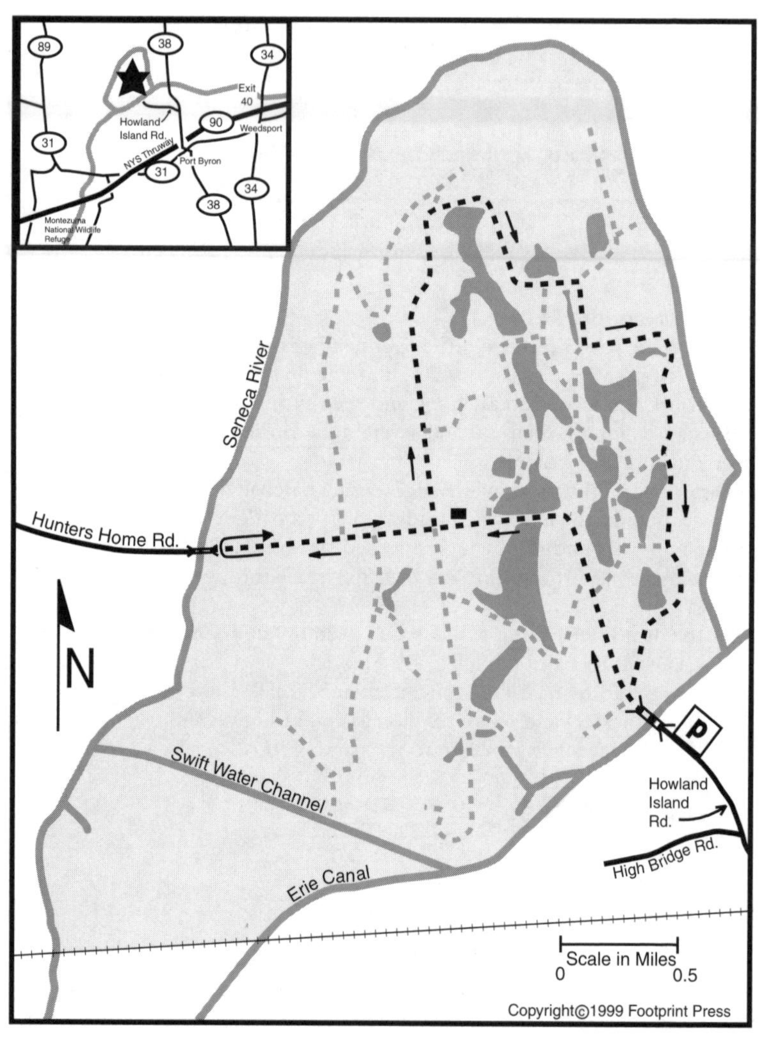

Howland Island

36.
Howland Island

Location: Three miles northwest of Port Byron, Cayuga County

Directions: From Port Byron (between exits 40 & 41 on the N.Y.S. Thruway) head north on Route 38. Turn west on Howland Island Road and follow it to the closed bridge. Park along the right side of the road, before the bridge.

Alternative Parking: At the west entrance on Hunters Home Road (an extension of Carn Cross Road)

Hiking Time: 4 hours

Biking Time: 2 hours

Length: 7.8 mile loop

Difficulty:

Surface: Dirt, gravel, and grass trails

Trail Markings: None

Uses: 

Dogs: OK

Admission: Free

Contact: Howland Island Wildlife Area
N.Y.S. Department Of Environmental Conservation
1285 Fisher Avenue
Cortland, NY 13045
(607) 753-3095
http://www.dec.state.ny.us

Waters of the Seneca River and the Erie (Barge) Canal surround the 3,100 acres of Howland Island. The land was first settled and cleared for farming in the 1800s, and farming continued until the 1920s. The land was purchased as a game refuge in 1932, and became a Civilian Conservation Corps (C.C.C.) camp between 1933 and 1941. The C.C.C. built 18 earthen dikes to create about 300 acres of water impoundments.

Riding the dikes on Howland Island.

The rolling hills and steep drumlins above these impoundments are now home to a second growth mixture of hardwoods, such as maple, ash, willow, basswood, black locust, oak, and hickory. The trails are abandoned gravel roads and old service vehicle tracks, now sufficiently packed to make pleasant biking trails. The route described here uses gravel roads for the predominately uphill section and packed grass trails for the predominately downhill section.

Through the 1930s and 1940s, Howland Island was home to an extensive pheasant farm operation that produced both eggs and pheasants. In 1951, a special waterfowl research project was begun to propagate duck species exotic to New York. Since 1962, the area has been managed for the natural production of waterfowl.

Hunting is allowed on portions of Howland Island so be sure to wear colorful clothing if you venture out during May or from mid-October through November. If you encounter signs saying "Baited Area, hunting or entry within posted area prohibited," you can ignore them. Personnel from the D.E.C. clarified that hunting is prohibited in these areas, but walking and bicycling are allowed.

Campground: Hejamada Family RV Park, RD 1 McDonald Road, Port Byron, (315) 776-5887

Hills and deep woodlands on Howland Island.

Trail Directions

- From Howland Island Road, ride across the bridge over the Erie Canal.
- Pass a grass trail to the right. (This will be part of your return loop.)
- At 0.7 mile, pass a trail to the right, then a grass trail to the left.

Continue straight on the gravel road.

- Pass a yellow metal gate at 0.9 mile.
- Reach a "T" and turn left.
- Pass lily ponds and head uphill.
- Pass a D.E.C. building and then pass an intersection.
- Climb another hill and pass a trail to the left.
- Pass a trail to the right.
- Reach a water channel, earthen bridge, and yellow barricade. (Beyond here is the alternate parking area.)
- Turn around and follow the gravel road back past two trail junctions.
- At the third trail, turn left on two gravel tracks.
- Pass a trail to the right.
- Bear right at a "Y."
- Pass a pond on the right.
- Ride between two ponds.
- Pass a trail on the right.
- At 3.7 miles, reach a "T" and turn right (S).
- At the next intersection, turn left off the gravel tracks, riding uphill on a grass trail.
- You'll enter a pleasant green tunnel and a long gradual downhill.
- Pass a pond.
- At 2.6 miles, reach a "Y" and bear left past a pond.
- Continue straight past a trail junction.
- Pass another pond.
- Pass a yellow metal gate.
- Reach the gravel road and turn left to cross the Erie canal bridge back to the parking area.

Date Bicycled: ______________

Notes:

The Erie Canal

The idea for the Erie Canal was born in our very own Finger Lakes area – in Canandaigua to be more precise. To be absolutely accurate; the idea was born in the Canandaigua jail, which at the time was the second floor of Sheriff Elijah Tilloson's hotel, The prisoner who dared to dream this grand folly was Jesse Hawley, a once wealthy businessman, besieged with debt from his less than lucrative freight forwarding business. Hawley had attempted to make a business out of moving flour and wheat from farms in the area to the Mynderse Mill at the falls on the Seneca River (now Seneca Falls), then to market in New York City. The land and water route available to him was difficult, dangerous, and costly. Using maps in the Canandaigua jail, Hawley sketched the route for a man-made waterway, linking Lake Erie to the Hudson River. He wrote fourteen articles detailing the concept, benefits, route, and cost for an idea that many ridiculed as "the effusions of a maniac."

In 1809, a member of the Ontario County legislature took the articles to Albany for investigation. Mayor of New York City, Dewitt Clinton, took up the cause. The canal became his political passion as he became Governor of New York. Ground was broken for the Erie Canal in 1817. Eight years later, the canal opened. American ingenuity overcame a multitude of obstacles along the way. America had no engineers or engineering schools in the early 1800s. Clinton asked a British engineer to head this project, but he declined the offer, forcing Clinton to use American leadership. The closest America had were lawyers who had some surveying experience. The canal became a huge on-the-job-training endeavor. It led to the development of the Rensselaer Polytechnic Institute in Troy, the Civil Engineering Department of Union College, and the Rochester Institute of Technology.

These inexperienced engineers had to devise ways to build locks, including ones to overcome the 60-foot rise of the Niagara Escarpment in Lockport. They had to develop waterproof cement, blast through bedrock, and build aqueducts, including the 804-foot long span over the Genesee River in downtown Rochester and the 1-mile span over the Irondequoit Valley in Pittsford. A challenge for the western end of the canal was how to keep enough water in the canal, especially during summer draughts. To accomplish this, feeders were built, rerouting water from lakes, streams, and reservoirs along the way into the canal.

Clinton's Folly, the original Erie Canal, was only 40 feet wide and 4 feet deep. But, it was an instant economic success. It shortened the transportation of goods between Buffalo and New York City from 6 weeks to 10 days and lowered the cost of transporting one ton of freight from $100 to $10. All of a sudden goods could move east to market and immigrants could move west to open land. Business boomed.

By 1835, the canal was log jammed with too much traffic. So, a major effort was undertaken to enlarge the Erie Canal. Locks were doubled to allow two-way traffic and lengthened to accommodate longer boats. The canal was straightened in various places to decrease its total length and it was widened to 70 feet and deepened to 7 feet. This second version of the Erie Canal is now known as the enlarged Erie Canal.

Over the years, additional work was done. In some areas, there was a second enlarged Erie Canal. But, the next major change came in 1918. The canal was once again over capacity. By now, technological know-how had improved. Engineers now knew how to incorporate the canal into existing rivers and control the water levels. The Erie Canal was once again enlarged and moved. This time it took over riverbeds such as the Clyde River and the Mohawk River. The new and improved version was renamed the Barge Canal.

In sections, for example, Lockport to Greece and Fairport to Palmyra, there is little difference in location of the three canals. With each enhancement, the ditch simply got larger. In other places, the three waterways had distinctly different locations, and all three can be seen today. The stretch from Port Byron through Jordan to Camillus is an example of the latter.

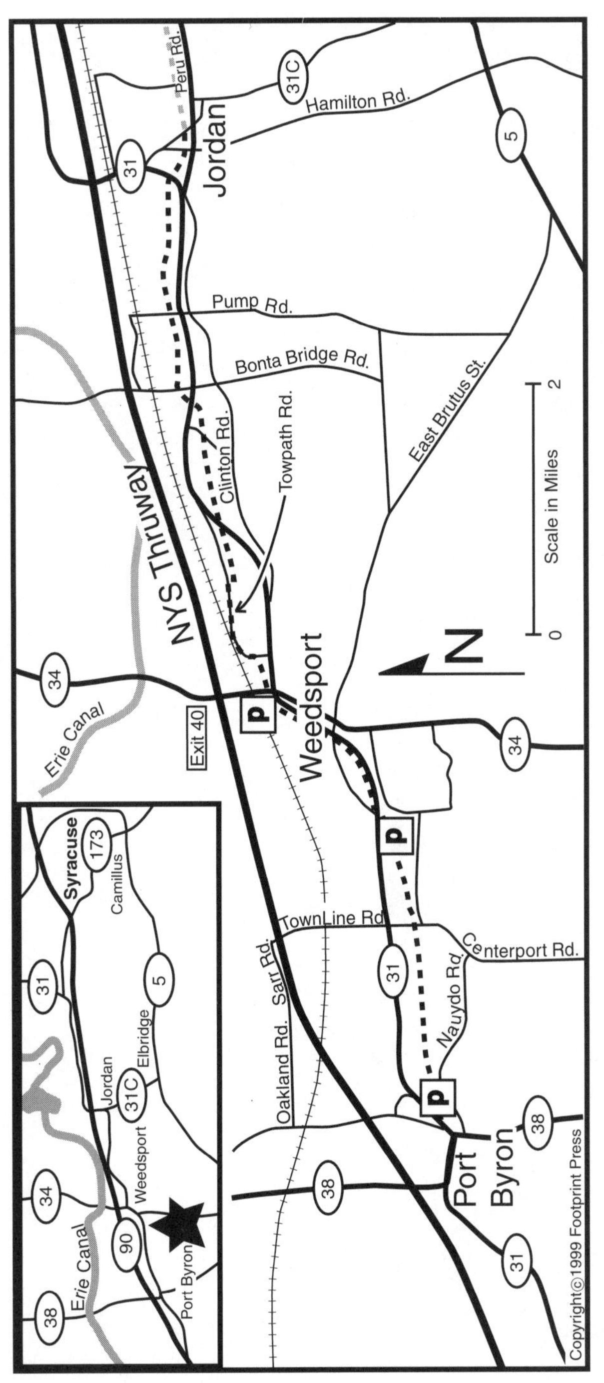

Cayuga County Erie Canal Trail (Port Byron to Jordan)

37.
Cayuga County Erie Canal Trail (Port Byron to Jordan)

Location: Port Byron, Weedsport, and Jordan (south of the N.Y.S. Thruway), Cayuga and Onondaga Counties

Directions: From Port Byron, head east on Route 3. Park in the canal bed at Randolph J. Schasel Village Park, on the south side of Route 31. A small brown-and-yellow sign, "Cayuga County Erie Canal Trail" is visible from Route 31.

Alternative Parking: Centerport Aqueduct Park, Route 31, west of Weedsport
North Main Street, Jordan, in front of Lock 51 Garden

Hiking Time: 5 hours

Biking Time: 2 hours

Length: 9.3 miles one way

Difficulty:

Surface: Dirt, gravel, and grass trail

Trail Markings: Some signs, "Cayuga County Erie Canal Trail"

Uses:

Dogs: OK

Admission: Free

Contact: County Planner
Cayuga County Planning Board
160 Genesee Street
Auburn, NY 13021-1276
(315) 253-1276

Michele Beilman
Cayuga County Parks and Trails Commission
East Lake Road
Auburn, N.Y. 13021
(315) 253-5611

The 1.5-mile section of enlarged Erie Canal that remains between Port Byron and Centerport was made accessible to the public in the fall of 1987. The Lock 52 Historical Society and concerned community members cleared the former towpath and canal bed to make the canal with its hand-placed stone sides visible.

The Randolph J. Schasel Village Park in Port Byron marks the beginning of this trail, which is built partly in the old canal bed and includes a pavilion, playground, and basketball court. Past Centerport, this trail becomes pretty rough. The trail bed includes gravel, mowed grass, weeds, and some roads. It continues through Weedsport to Jordan. The trail actually continues another 14.8 miles through Erie Canal Park in Camillus (see Trails #38 and #39).

Weedsport derived its name from the Weed brothers, Edward and Elihu, who dug and founded Weed's Basin, a re-supply point on the original Erie Canal.

Bed and Breakfast:	The Mansard B&B, Weedsport, (315) 834-2262
Campgrounds:	Hejamada Family RV Park, RD 1 McDonald Road, Port Byron, (315) 776-5887
	Riverforest Park, 2526 Riverforest Road, Weedsport, (315) 834-9458

Trail Directions

- From the parking area, head east on the trail between Route 31 and the basketball court. The enlarged Erie Canal will be on your right. Further to the right is the original Clinton's Ditch.
- At 0.9 mile, pass the Harring Brook receiver. All the water from this creek dumped into the canal.
- Cross Centerport Road.
- Cross a wooden bridge. Centerport Aqueduct will be on the right. It was built in 1835 to carry the canal over Cold Spring Brook. There is a rare dam in the creek next to the aqueduct.
- At 2.4 miles, reach Centerport Aqueduct Park and Route 31. (Parking is available here.)
- Turn right and follow Route 31 for 1.5 miles to Route 34.
- Cross Route 31 to Arby's. The trail continues behind Arby's.
- Pass the brown sign for "Cayuga County Erie Canal Trail."
- Cross a wooden bridge over Putnum Brook then pass a pond and pen,

home to ducks, geese, turkeys, and chickens.

- At 4.1 miles, reach Towpath Road and turn left.
- Follow Towpath Road for 0.7 mile. The trail begins again on the right, after a chained gate into the back of Cayuga County Fairgrounds. There are no signs and no parking area, simply a mowed grass path, heading southeast.
- Turn right onto the trail. You will be in a pleasant woods "tunnel" with the old canal to your left and a creek to your right.
- At 5.6 miles, cross Route 31 and bear left. (The trail to the right returns to Weedsport, Route 31B.)
- The trail will get rough. Watch carefully for woodchuck holes.
- Cross Lippoldt Road.
- At 6.5 miles, cross Route 31 again.
- Cross Bonta Bridge Road. The trail bed will improve.
- Cross Pump Road. The enlarged Erie Canal is again on your right.
- Pass a double lock from the enlarged Erie Canal on your right.
- Cross a farm lane. The trail turns from gravel to dirt with roots.
- At 8.7 miles, cross Route 31. The trail continues in the woods behind a sign, "Jordan-Elbridge Area Church Board."
- Cross through a mowed field. The back of the Jordan Diner will be to your left.
- Cross Werner Way then cross the grass behind the fire hall.
- Cross Hamilton Road.
- Immediately in front of you will be a park. Cross the park on the mowed grass inside the old canal bed until you reach North Main Street, Jordan. (Parking is available along North Main Street.) You've come 9.3 miles.
  [Continue straight on the path between Lock 51 Garden and the Masonic Lodge to connect with the Erie Canalway Trail #38 (Jordan to Camillus), for a 20-mile ride.]

Date Bicycled: ______________

Notes:

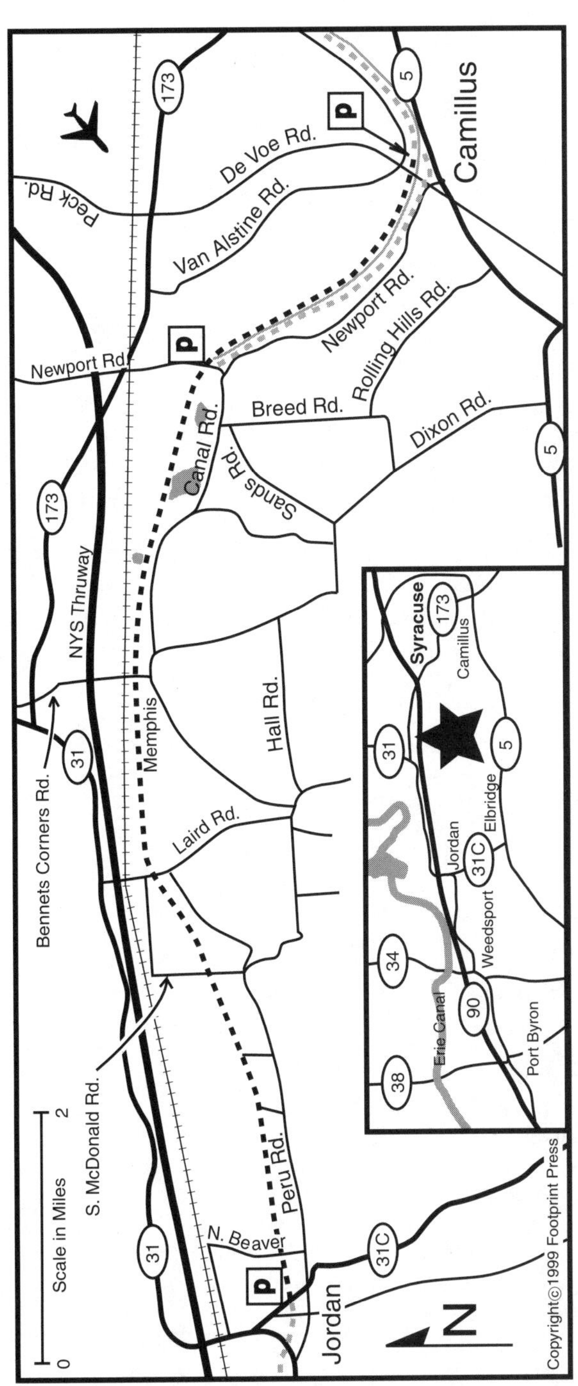

Erie Canalway Trail (Jordan to Camillus)

38.
Erie Canalway Trail (Jordan to Camillus)

Location:	Jordan to Camillus, Onondaga County
Directions:	Park along North Main Street (Route 31C), Jordan, in front of Lock 51 Garden (between the Laundromat and Masonic Lodge).
Alternative Parking:	Town of Camillus Erie Canal Park, Newport Road Camillus Erie Canal Park, Devoe Road
Hiking Time:	5.5 hours
Biking Time:	2.5 hours
Length:	10.8 miles one way
Difficulty:	
Surface:	Dirt and gravel trail
Trail Markings:	None
Uses:	 
Dogs:	OK
Admission:	Free
Contact:	P.O. Box 397 Jordan, NY 13080 (315) 689-3278

Also called the Erie Canal Parkway, this is an easy-to-follow, well-maintained trail along the abandoned enlarged Erie Canal.

Trail Directions

- Head east along the path between Lock 51 Garden and the Masonic Lodge.
- Pass North Beaver Street as you ride through Old Erie Place Park. Picnic tables and parking are available here.
- The enlarged Erie Canal will appear on your right.
- Pass a road on the right.
- Pass Schapp Road.
- Reach the waste weir on the left. This is where water from Carpenter Brook was used to help control the level of water in the Erie Canal.
- Cross South McDonald Road in Peru.
- Pass a private house and the McIntyre, a former hotel along the canal,

The abandoned canal bed is now Lock 51 Garden in Jordan.

Remains of an aqueduct used to carry the canal over Carpenter Brook.

as you approach Laird Road. You've come 4.2 miles.

- At 5.8 miles, cross Bennets Corners Road at the town of Memphis.
- Cross under power lines.
- Pass a gravel road to the right. The trail becomes a gravel and paved roadway.
- At 8.6 miles, cross Newport Road. The Brown Cow Café is on this corner. Across the road, enter the Town of Camillus Erie Canal Project. (Parking is available here.)
- Pass the Camillus Sportsman's Club.
- Cross Devoe Road into Camillus Erie Canal Park. (Parking is available here.) You've come 10.8 miles.
  [Continue to Trail #39 for an additional 8.5 mile loop.]

Date Bicycled: _______________
Notes:

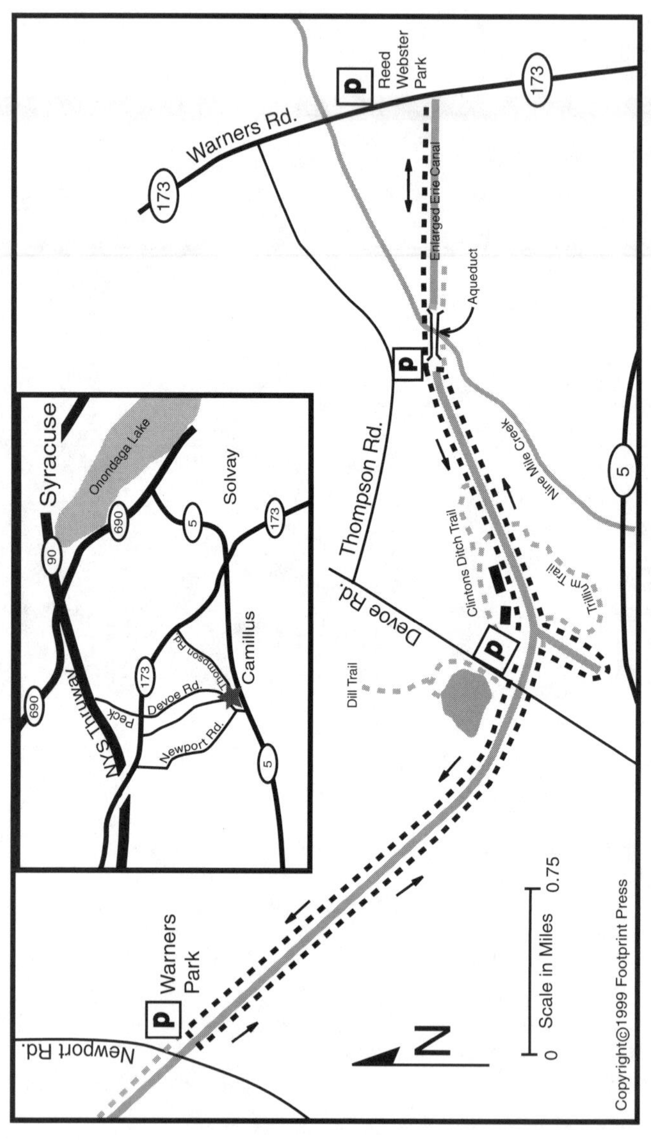

Erie Canal Park

39.
Erie Canal Park

Location: Camillus (west of Syracuse), Onondaga County
Directions: From Route 5, turn north on Devoe Road. Erie Canal Park is on the right, just south of Thompson Road.
Alternative Parking: Warners Park on Newport Road
Reed Webster Park on Warners Road
A parking area off Thompson Road, near the dock and aqueduct
Hiking Time: 4.5 hours
Biking Time: 1.75 hours
Length: 8.5-mile loop
Difficulty:
Surface: Dirt and gravel trail
Trail Markings: None
Uses:
Dogs: OK on leash
Admission: Free
Contacts: Town of Camillus Erie Canal Park
David Beebe, Director Sims' Museum
109 East Way
Camillus, NY 13031
(315) 488-3409

Camillus Town Hall
4600 West Genesee Street
Syracuse, NY 13219
(315) 488-1234

The enlarged Erie Canal was abandoned in 1922. It sat idle until 1972, when the Town of Camillus purchased a seven-mile stretch. Since then, an army of volunteers has been busy clearing the land, building dams, refilling the canal with water, and building a replica of Sims' store. The original Sims' store was built in 1856, at the intersection of Warners Road and the canal. It served as a general store, home for the Sims family, and as a depar-

Handcrafted stone walls are still visible along this section of the abandoned canal.

ture point for persons boarding the canal boats. The store was destroyed by fire in 1863, but the replica lives on today. The first floor is set up like the original store. The second floor houses exhibits and antiques of the era along with models of locks, aqueducts, and canal boats. Sims' Museum is open on Saturdays from 9:00 AM until 1:00 PM year-round and on Sundays from 1:00 until 5:00 PM, May through October, and 1:00 until 4:00 PM, November through April.

The trails are available year-round during daylight hours. This trail circumnavigates the historic enlarged Erie Canal and passes sections of the original Clinton's Ditch. Rain shelters are built at several locations along the trail. It's an easy bicycle loop, perfect for family outings.

The volunteers of Town of Camillus Erie Canal Park & Sims' Store Museum plan to reconstruct the aqueduct in 1999, and to complete the trail along the south side of the canal from the aqueduct to Warners Road (Route 173). This renovation will enable riders to continue on the south side of the canal past the aqueduct, cross over at Warners Road, and return on the north side of the canal for a nice loop.

Bed & Breakfasts:	B&B Wellington, 707 Danforth Street, Syracuse, (315) 474-3641
	Green Gate Inn, 2 Genesee Street, Camillus, (315) 672-9276
Boat Tours:	Canal Boat Tours are offered Sundays, May through October, from 1:00 until 5:00 PM. Cost is $1.50 for children and $3 for adults. Dinner cruises are also offered. Call (315) 488-3409 for details.
Ice Cream:	Village of Camillus Sunoco Gas Station, corner Main Street (West Genesee Street) and Newport Road (seasonal)

Trail Directions

- From the parking area at Sims' Store, ride west across Devoe Road, following the northeast side of the enlarged Erie Canal. The path is paved for 0.7 mile.
- Pass a barricade and continue straight on a dirt path.
- At 2.1 miles, before a gate to Warners Park, turn left then left again to return on the opposite side of the canal.
- Pass a sign showing where the enlarged Erie Canal crossed Clinton's

Riding the original towpath parallel to the aqueduct supports which carried the canal over Nine Mile Creek.

Ditch.

- At 4.2 miles, cross Devoe Road and continue straight.
- At the pedestrian bridge turn right on the West Feeder Trail.
- Reach the end of the feeder and turn left around its end to return on the opposite side.
- Reach the canal and turn right.
- Pass the entrance to Trillium Trail (hikers only).
- Pass the exit of Trillium Trail.
- Reach the dock at 5.6 miles. (Straight ahead leads to a dead end at the aqueduct. A parking area is to the left on Thompson Road.) Turn left then turn right immediately to continue riding on the other side of the canal, still heading east.
- Cross the towpath next to the aqueduct that once carried canal waters over Nine Mile Creek. All that remains are the stone supports for the wooden trough.
- Reach Warners Road (Route 173) at 6.6 miles. (Parking is available across the street in Reed Webster Park.)
- Turn around and retrace your path back past the aqueduct.
- Continue straight past the dock and parking area on Thompson Road.
- Pass the culvert, which carried runoff water under the canal to Nine Mile Creek.
- Return to the parking area at Sims' Museum.

Date Bicycled: _______________

Notes:

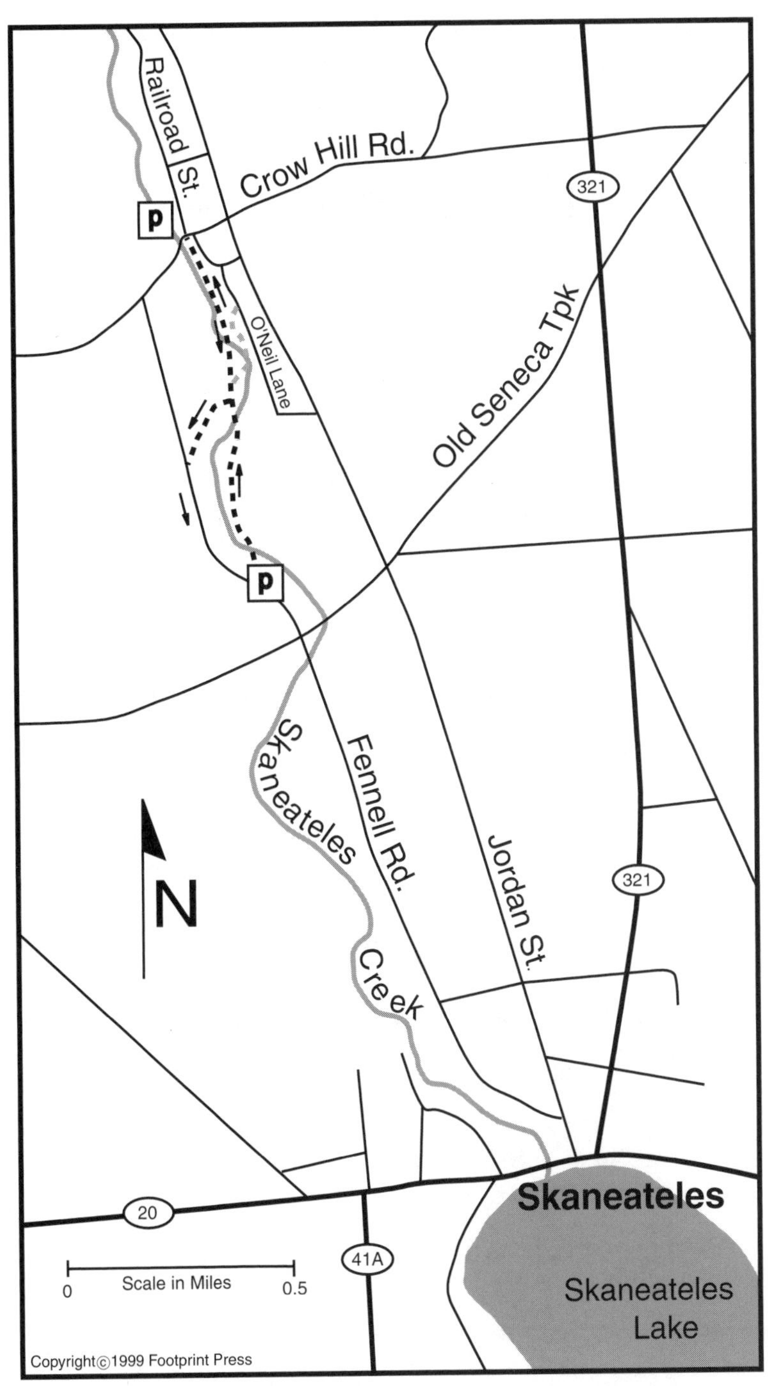

Charlie Major Nature Trail

40.
Charlie Major Nature Trail

Location: North of the village of Skaneateles, Onondaga County

Directions: From Route 20 in Skaneateles, turn north onto Jordan Street, then left onto Fennell Road. Look for a gravel parking area, 500-feet north of Old Seneca Turnpike, on the east side of Fennel Road. A gray sign with black lettering "Nature Trail" marks the area.

Alternative Parking: A parking area on Crow Hill Road near the corner of Railroad Street

Hiking Time: 50 minutes

Biking Time: 20 minutes

Length: 1.6 mile loop

Difficulty:

Surface: Dirt and crushed stone trail

Trail Markings: None

Uses: 

Dogs: OK

Admission: Free

Contact: Town of Skaneateles
24 Jordan Street
Skaneateles, NY 13152
(315) 685-3473

The Charlie Major Nature Trail was named after Charles T. Major, Jr., a public figure who featured prominently in the history and development of this rail trail. Mr. Major served as village justice, town justice, town board member, and town supervisor from the 1950s through the 1990s, often taking town employees on nature walks to this obscure place which had featured prominently in the area's history. The nature trail was his idea. Today he is a state supreme court justice.

The early settlers, arriving in the area beginning in 1794, recognized that the drop of 100 feet in the flow of water down the Skaneateles outlet from

Skaneateles Lake north would furnish water power for industry. This cheap source of waterpower gave rise to the bustling community of Mottville. A railroad for horse-drawn cars was built along the creek in 1840, followed by a plank road which was used only a few years. Then, the steam railroad came in 1866. Sawmills, gristmills, tanneries, woolen mills, distilleries, and paper mills dotted the waterfront. As these industries declined, the factories became the sites for the manufacture of vacuum cleaners, cement blocks, tiles, chemicals, and medical instruments.

Remains of this industrial era can be seen along the trail today. Parts of the dam and headrace from Mottville Woodworking Factory are on the side trail heading up to O'Neil Lane. This factory was originally a power plant, then a woodworking factory that made tools for farmers by 1826. Also visible are stone ruins from Morton's Woolen Mill, which began in 1800 as a sawmill, gristmill, and distillery. This mill was built into a factory in 1852. In 1862, uniforms for Union soldiers were made here under the name Mottville Woolen Mill. The mill closed in 1890, and burned in 1894.

When the city of Syracuse began using the water from Skaneateles Lake for its drinking water, it took over control of the dam at the outlet. The water level in the creek was lowered below a level necessary for mill operations, so other methods of power generation had to be sought. At one point, so little water flowed down the Skaneateles outlet that the sewage concentration became high enough to initiate an outbreak of typhoid. A second epidemic swept the area in the 1920s, when well water became contaminated. Charles Major, Senior, was responsible for organizing a town committee to bring piped water to the community.

The rail line, eventually known as the Short Line, helped to maintain prosperity in the community by serving the industries along the outlet. It also carried passengers from the New York Central Railroad at Skaneateles Junction to Skaneateles where they could board the steamboats for trips around the lake. Today, the rails are gone and a serene path follows Skaneateles Creek for part of its journey, as it flows northward from Skaneateles Lake into the Seneca River. The trail is equally pleasant as a walk or a bike ride.

Bed & Breakfasts: Fox Ridge Farm B&B, Skaneateles, (315) 673-4881

The Gray House, 47 Jordan Street, Skaneateles, (315) 685-5224

Hobbit Hollow Farm B&B, 3061 West Lake Road, Skaneateles, (315) 685-2791

Lady of the Lake B&B, 2 West Lake Street, Skaneateles, (888) 685-7997

Millard's at the Summit B&B, Route 41, Skaneateles, (315) 673-2254

Sherwood Inn, 26 West Genesee Street, Skaneateles, (315) 685-3405

Trail Directions

- From the parking area on Fennel Road, head northwest on the trail.
- Cross a wooden bridge over Skaneateles Creek.
- The creek will now be on your left, parallel to the trail.
- Cross a second bridge.
- At 0.3 mile, reach a "Y" intersection. (The trail to the left goes for 0.12 mile to Fennel Road.) Continue straight (S).
- Immediately after a brick shed is a trail to the right. Notice the dam in the creek to the right. (The trail to the right heads uphill for 0.13 mile to O'Neil Lane, past the dam, and crosses the old mill race of Mottville Woodworking Factory.) Continue straight.
- At 0.5 mile, cross a bridge over the creek.
- Reach Crow Hill Road at 0.8 mile. Turn around and ride back on the same path.
- When the trail comes to a "Y," bear right.
- Turn left onto Fennel Road and ride the road back to the parking area.

Date Bicycled: ____________

Notes:

Definitions

Aqueduct: A stone, wood, or cement trough built to carry canal waters over an existing creek or river. At the time, the world's largest aqueduct was built in Rochester to span the Genesee River. Eleven stone arches were erected, spanning 800 feet, to withstand the annual floods of this wild river.

Ballast: Broken stone used as a base for a railroad bed.

Bog: An acid-rich, wet, poorly drained, spongy area characterized by plants such as sedges, heaths, and sphagnum.

Carding: Combing of wool.

Corduroy: A method of spanning a wet section of trail by laying logs perpendicular to the trail. This creates a bumpy effect like corduroy material.

Deciduous: Describes trees that loose their leaves in winter.

Drumlin: An elongated or oval hill created from glacial debris.

Esker: A ridge of debris formed when a river flowed under the glacier in an icy tunnel. Rocky material accumulated on the tunnel beds, and when the glacier melted, a ridge of rubble remained.

Feeder: A diverted stream, brook, or other water source used to maintain water the level in the canal.

Fulling Mill: A mill for cleaning wool and producing cloth.

Gristmill: A mill for grinding grain into flour.

Headrace: A trough or tunnel for conveying water to a point of industrial application.

Impoundments: Areas of marshland and ponds created by man-made earthen dikes.

Jewelweed: Also called touch-me-not, this plant is a member of the impatiens family. It grows in moist areas with a translucent stem and small snapdragon-like flowers in yellow, orange, or pink. The leaves shine silvery under water, hence the name jewelweed. The crushed plant has historically been used as a treatment for poison ivy, but recent studies show that it's not effective.

Lady's Slipper: This perennial herb has a pouch-like flower that resembles a dainty slipper. A victim of habitat destruction and over collection, this rare beauty is fast disappearing.

Leatherleaf: A shrub that grows on top of sphagnum moss and allows other plants to gain a foot hold. It produces white, bell-like flowers in spring.

Marsh: An area of soft, wet land.

Mule: The sterile offspring of a male donkey and a female horse. Mules were often used to pull boats along the Erie Canal.

Purple Loosestrife: An aggressive perennial carried from Europe in the ballast holds of ships. These blazing magenta flowering plants are spreading across American wetlands and crowding out native plants. The name is derived from the early practice of placing this plant over the yoke of quarrelsome oxen. The plant was said to help the oxen "loose their strife" or quiet down.

Sawmill: A mill for cutting trees into lumber.

Sphagnum Moss: A type of moss that grows in swamps and has an incredible capacity to hold water. It's estimated that this moss can soak up more than 100 times its own weight in water. In bogs where acids build up and oxygen is lacking, the moss compresses rather than degrades and forms peat. Dried, shredded, and packed in bales, sphagnum moss is sold as peat moss and is used by gardeners to retain moisture in soil.

Swamp: Wet, spongy land saturated and sometimes partially or intermittently covered with water.

Switchbacks: Winding the trail back and forth across the face of a steep area to make the incline more gradual.

Waste Weir: A dam along the side of the canal that allows overflow water to dissipate to a side waterway.

Trails Under 4 Miles

Page	Trail Name	Length (miles)
50	Silver Lake Outlet	0.8
191	Casey Park	1.0
213	Charlie Major Nature Trail	1.6
45	Genesee County Park & Forest – Inner Loop	1.8
188	Auburn – Fleming Trail	2.0
173	East Ithaca Recreation Way	2.2
95	Victor – Lehigh Valley Trail	2.8
41	Genesee County Park & Forest – Outer Loop	2.9
115	Harriet Hollister Spencer Memorial State Recreation Area – Sidewinder Trail	3.3
105	Ontario Pathways Trail	3.4
181	Bear Swamp State Forest – Short Loop	3.4
111	Canadice Lake Trail	3.7

Trails 5 to 7 Miles

Page	Trail Name	Length (miles)
41 & 45	Genesee County Park & Forest – Inner & Outer Loops	4.7
78	Rattlesnake Hill – Bike Loop	5.0
84	Genesee Valley Greenway – Scottsville	5.1
138	Canal Park Trailway	5.8
53	Letchworth State Park – Trout Pond Loop	6.1
124	Middlesex Valley Rail Trail	6.8
154	Sugar Hill State Forest	6.8
159	Queen Catherine Marsh	7.0
169	South Hill Recreation Way	7.0
99	Auburn Trail	7.5
129	Keuka Lake Outlet Trail	7.5
33	Oak Orchard Wildlife Management Area	7.8
185	Bear Swamp State Forest – Long Loop	7.8
194	Howland Island	7.8

Trails 8 - 11 Miles

Page	Trail Name	Length (miles)
81	Rattlesnake Hill – Linear Bike Trail	8.4
176	Dryden Lake Park Trail	8.4
208	Erie Canal Park	8.5
119	Lakeshore Park / Seneca Lake State Park	9.0
164	Connecticut Hill Wildlife Management Area	9.1
201	Cayuga County Erie Canal Trail (Port Byron to Jordan)	9.3
142	Sampson State Park – Lake Trail	9.4
60	Letchworth State Park – Big Bend Loop	9.5
65	Genesee Valley Greenway – Portageville to Nunda	9.5
205	Erie Canalway Trail (Jordan to Camillus)	10.8
181 & 185	Bear Swamp State Forest – Short & Long Loops	11.2

Trails Over 12 Miles

Page	Trail Name	Length (miles)
29	Iroquois National Wildlife Refuge and Tonawanda Wildlife Management Area	12.5
89	Mendon – Lehigh Valley Trail	12.5
71	Genesee Valley Greenway – Cuylerville to Avon	12.6
78 & 81	Rattlesnake Hill – Linear and Loop Bike Trails	13.0
47	Groveland Secondary	13.3
89 & 95	Mendon and Victor – Lehigh Valley Trails	15.0
65 & 60	Genesee Valley Greenway – Portageville to Nunda and Letchworth State Park – Big Bend Loop	19.0
99 & 89 & 95	Auburn Trail and Mendon and Victor – Lehigh Valley Trails	22.0
148	Finger Lakes National Forest	25.1
201 & 205 & 208	Cayuga County Erie Canal Trail, Erie Canalway Trail and Erie Canal Park	28.6

1 Boot Trails

Page	Trail Name	Difficulty (boots)
50	Silver Lake Outlet	1
84	Genesee Valley Greenway – Scottsville	1
95	Victor – Lehigh Valley Trail	1
99	Auburn Trail	1
105	Ontario Pathways Trail	1
111	Canadice Lake Trail	1
119	Lakeshore Park / Seneca Lake State Park	1
159	Queen Catherine Marsh	1
176	Dryden Lake Park Trail	1
188	Auburn – Fleming Trail	1
201	Cayuga County Erie Canal Trail (Port Byron to Jordan)	1
205	Erie Canalway Trail (Jordan to Camillus)	1
208	Erie Canal Park	1
213	Charlie Major Nature Trail	1

2 Boot Trails

Page	Trail Name	Difficulty (boots)
29	Iroquois National Wildlife Refuge and Tonawanda Wildlife Management Area	2
33	Oak Orchard Wildlife Management Area	2
47	Groveland Secondary	2
71	Genesee Valley Greenway – Cuylerville to Avon	2
81	Rattlesnake Hill – Linear Bike Trail	2
124	Middlesex Valley Rail Trail	2
129	Keuka Lake Outlet Trail	2
169	South Hill Recreation Way	2
173	East Ithaca Recreation Way	2
191	Casey Park	2

3 Boot Trails

Page	Trail Name	Difficulty (boots)
60	Letchworth State Park – Big Bend Loop	3
78	Rattlesnake Hill – Bike Loop	3
89	Mendon – Lehigh Valley Trail	3

3 Boot Trails

Page	Trail Name	Difficulty (boots)
115	Harriet Hollister Spencer Memorial State Recreation Area – Sidewinder Trail	3
138	Canal Park Trailway	3
142	Sampson State Park – Lake Trail	3
181	Bear Swamp State Forest – Short Loop	3
194	Howland Island	3

4 Boot Trails

Page	Trail Name	Difficulty (boots)
41	Genesee County Park & Forest – Outer Loop	4
45	Genesee County Park & Forest – Inner Loop	4
53	Letchworth State Park – Trout Pond Loop	4
65	Genesee Valley Greenway – Portageville to Nunda	4
148	Finger Lakes National Forest	4
154	Sugar Hill State Forest	4
164	Connecticut Hill Wildlife Management Area	4
185	Bear Swamp State Forest – Long Loop	4

Trails Where a Mountain Bike is Recommended

Page	Trail Name	Difficulty (boots)
53	Letchworth State Park – Trout Pond Loop	4
65	Genesee Valley Greenway – Portageville to Nunda	4
89	Mendon – Lehigh Valley Trail	3
154	Sugar Hill State Forest	4
181	Bear Swamp State Forest – Short Loop	3
185	Bear Swamp State Forest – Long Loop	4

Paved Trails

Page	Trail Name	Difficulty (boots)
119	Lakeshore Park / Seneca Lake State Park	1
142	Sampson State Park – Lake Trail	3
173	East Ithaca Recreation Way	2
191	Casey Park	2

Loop Trails

Page	Trail Name	Length (miles)
191	Casey Park	1.0
213	Charlie Major Nature Trail	1.6
45	Genesee County Park & Forest – Inner Loop	1.8
41	Genesee County Park & Forest – Outer Loop	2.9
115	Harriet Hollister Spencer Memorial State Recreation Area – Sidewinder Trail	3.3
181	Bear Swamp State Forest – Short Loop	3.4
78	Rattlesnake Hill – Bike Loop	5.0
53	Letchworth State Park – Trout Pond Loop	6.1
154	Sugar Hill State Forest	6.8
159	Queen Catherine Marsh	7.0
33	Oak Orchard Wildlife Management Area	7.8
185	Bear Swamp State Forest – Long Loop	7.8
194	Howland Island	7.8
208	Erie Canal Park	8.5
119	Lakeshore Park / Seneca Lake State Park	9.0
164	Connecticut Hill Wildlife Management Area	9.1
142	Sampson State Park – Lake Trail	9.4
60	Letchworth State Park – Big Bend Loop	9.5
29	Iroquois National Wildlife Refuge and Tonawanda Wildlife Management Area	12.5
148	Finger Lakes National Forest	25.1

Linear Trails

Page	Trail Name	Length (miles)
50	Silver Lake Outlet	0.8
188	Auburn – Fleming Trail	2.0
173	East Ithaca Recreation Way	2.2
95	Victor – Lehigh Valley Trail	2.8
105	Ontario Pathways Trail	3.4
111	Canadice Lake Trail	3.7
84	Genesee Valley Greenway – Scottsville	5.1
138	Canal Park Trailway	5.8
124	Middlesex Valley Rail Trail	6.8

Linear Trails

Page	Trail Name	Length (miles)
169	South Hill Recreation Way	7.0
99	Auburn Trail	7.5
129	Keuka Lake Outlet Trail	7.5
81	Rattlesnake Hill – Linear Bike Trail	8.4
176	Dryden Lake Park Trail	8.4
201	Cayuga County Erie Canal Trail (Port Byron to Jordan)	9.3
65	Genesee Valley Greenway – Portageville to Nunda	9.5
205	Erie Canalway Trail (Jordan to Camillus)	10.8
89	Mendon – Lehigh Valley Trail	12.5
71	Genesee Valley Greenway – Cuylerville to Avon	12.6
47	Groveland Secondary	13.3

References

Finger Lakes Association
309 Lake Street
Penn Yan, NY 14527
(800) KIT4FUN

Finger Lakes Interpretive Center
82 Seneca Street
P.O. Box 207
Geneva, NY 14456
(315) 789-1431

Genesee Valley Cycling Club
Neil J. Rowe
57 S. Beacon Hills Drive
Penfield, NY 14526
(716) 359-0124

G&T Athletics Cycling Club
(716) 234-2659

Lake Country Bike & Ski Club
124 North brook Street
Geneva, NY 14456
(315) 789-1138

Pedal Power
Huggers Ski Club
PO Box 23921
Rochester, NY 14692-3921
(716) 865-7910

Rails-to-Trails Conservancy
1400 Sixteenth Street NW
Suite 300
Washington, DC 20036
(202) 797-5400

Rochester Bicycling Club, Inc.
P.O. Box 10100
Rochester, NY 14610-0100
(716) 723-2953
http://www.win.net/~rbcbbs

Western New York Mountain
Biking Association
P.O. Box 1691
Amherst, NY 14226-7691

The authors, Rich and Sue Freeman decided to make their living from what they love – hiking and bicycling. In 1996 they left corporate jobs to spend six months hiking 2,200 miles on the Appalachian Trail from Georgia to Maine. That adventure deepened their love of the outdoors and inspired them to share this love by introducing others to the joys of hiking.

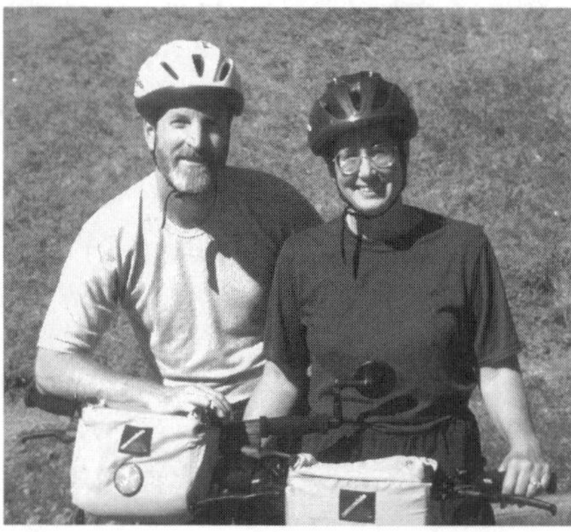

Since most people don't have the option (let alone the desire) to undertake a six-month trek, they decided to focus on short hikes, near home. The result was *Take A Hike! Family Walks in the Rochester Area* which described hikes around Rochester, N.Y. In researching this book, the Freemans' got to more fully explore the wonderful Finger Lakes and Genesee Valley Region.

Rich and Sue have been active members of Victor Hiking Trails since its inception. They continue to do trail work and participate with other local trail groups as well. In addition, their passion for long distance hiking continues. In 1997 they thru-hiked the 500-mile long Bruce Trail in Ontario, Canada. Future hikes include a segment of the Florida Trail and traversing 500 miles of the Pacific Crest Trail through the state of Washington.

Since beginning their new career writing and publishing books, the Freeman's have pared down their living expenses and are enjoying a simpler lifestyle. They now have control of their own destiny and the freedom to head into the woods for a refreshing respite when the urge strikes. Still, their life is infinitely more cluttered than when they carried all their wordly needs on their backs for six months on the Appalachian Trail.

Other Books Available from Footprint Press

***Take A Hike!** Family Walks in the Rochester Area*

ISBN# 0-9656974-60 U.S. $16.95 Can. $21.95

From parks to little known areas, this book describes 40 hikes within a 15 mile radius of Rochester, N.Y. Take the kids and dog along to explore the bounty of nature. Each trail has a map, description, and details you'll need such as where to park, estimated hiking time, and interesting things to see along the way.

***Take A Hike!** Family Walks in the Finger Lakes & Genesee Valley Region*

ISBN# 0-9656974-95 U.S. $16.95 Can. $21.95

Perfect for an afternoon walk, ramble, or hike on 51 trails through forests, glens, and bogs of upstate New York. Each trail has a map, description, and details you'll need such as where to park, estimated hiking time, and interesting points along the way.

***Take Your Bike!** Family Rides in the Rochester Area*

ISBN# 0-9656974-28 U.S. $16.95 Can. $21.95

Converted railroad beds, paved bike paths, woods trails, and little used country roads combine to create the 30 bicycle adventures within an easy drive of Rochester, N.Y. No need to have a mountain bike – any sturdy bicycle will do.

***Bruce Trail** – An Adventure Along the Niagara Escarpment*

ISBN# 0-9656974-36 U.S. $16.95 Can. $21.95

Come along as experienced backpackers take you on a five-week journey along the Niagara Escarpment in Ontario, Canada. Explore the now abandoned Welland Canal routes, caves formed by crashing waves, ancient cedar forests, and white cobblestone beaches along azure Georgian Bay. Learn the secrets of long-distance backpackers. As an armchair traveler or in preparation for a hike of your own, you'll enjoy this ramble along a truly unique part of North America.

***Alter** – A Simple Path to Emotional Wellness*

ISBN# 0-9656974-87 U.S. $16.95 Can. $21.95

Alter is a self-help manual which assists in recognizing and changing your emotional blocks and limiting belief systems. It uses easy-to-learn techniques of biofeedback to retrieve subliminal information and achieve personal transformation.

For sample maps and chapters explore our web site at:

http://www.footprintpress.com

Yes, I'd like to order Footprint Press Books:

\#

____ ***Take A Hike!*** *Family Walks in the Rochester Area*

____ ***Take A Hike!*** *Family Walks in the Finger Lakes & Genesee Valley Region*

____ ***Take Your Bike!*** *Family Rides in the Rochester Area*

____ ***Take Your Bike!*** *Family Rides in the Finger Lakes & Genesee Valley Region*

____ ***Bruce Trail*** *– An Adventure Along the Niagara Escarpment*

____ ***Alter*** *– A Simple Path to Emotional Wellness*

____ Total Books @ $16.95 US or $21.95 Canadian each

For 1 or 2 books, add $3 per book for tax and shipping.
For 3 or more books, FREE (tax and shipping will be included in book price)

Total enclosed: $______________

Your Name: ____

Address: ____

City: ______________________ State (Province): ______________

Zip (Postal Code): ______________________ Country: _________

Make check payable and mail to:
Footprint Press
P.O. Box 645
Fishers, N.Y. 14453

Or, check the web site at http://www.footprintpress.com

Footprint Press books are available at special discounts when purchased in bulk for sales promotions, premiums, or fund raising.